CHESHIRE
STEAM
COUNTY *of* CONTRASTS

DAVID PACKER

The
History
Press

First published 2009

The History Press
The Mill, Brimscombe Port
Stroud, Gloucestershire, GL5 2QG
www.thehistorypress.co.uk

British Library Cataloguing in Publication Data.
A catalogue record for this book is available from the British Library.

ISBN 978 0 7509 4678 0

Typesetting and origination by The History Press
Printed in Great Britain

Contents

Introduction

I have made an assertion that Cheshire is a county of contrasts because whether looking at its topography, its land uses or its railways and locomotives, one can see contrasting aspects. A common view of Cheshire is that it is a large low-lying plain and while that is a reasonably accurate description of much of the county, there are isolated hills too, and a mass of uplands along the eastern edge of the county. There is a small coastline and estuaries around the Wirral to add further variety.

In terms of land use, Cheshire is predominantly an agricultural county but it is probably best known for its salt deposits below the fields that support dairy farming. The presence of the salt industry was a major factor in the growth of the chemical industry, where salt was used in the manufacture of soap and paints, for instance. On the Wirral, shipbuilding was established in the nineteenth century and, further down the peninsula, William Lever established his soap factory at Port Sunlight. Cheshire had its share of the more traditional industries such as textiles on the eastern side of the county, from Congleton in the south to Stalybridge in the north, while in more limited areas of east Cheshire, coal was worked. The arrival of the railway brought new employment opportunities, especially at Crewe where the works was established.

Land uses, naturally, have had a vital bearing on the development of the railways; a classic example is the network around Northwich, following the growth of the salt and chemical industries nearby. Shipbuilding and docks facilities on the Wirral led to the development of dedicated rail networks around Birkenhead and locomotives suitable for working along lines with sharp curvature. The demographic pattern has had a big impact on railway development, especially to the south of Manchester, and on the Wirral, where suburban routes were built to carry passengers to and from work. Trade and industrial patterns outside the county have also influenced railway development. For instance, the desire of the railway companies to reach Manchester, Liverpool and the ports has, arguably, played a bigger role than any other factor in determining the course of many railways. It is most unlikely that the Great Western, the Manchester, Sheffield & Lincolnshire Railway or the Midland Railway would have passed through Cheshire without the temptation of the financial returns from the potential business in the cities.

In fact, Cheshire can be seen as a transport corridor, a conduit through which barges, trains and motor vehicles have passed through on their way to their destinations. Hemmed in by the Pennines to the east and the sea to the north-west, Cheshire has seen Roman roads, canals, railways and motorways passing through as well as serving the more local areas.

At this point it is worth clarifying the borders of the county for the purposes of this book. The Cheshire of the steam age was the familiar teapot shape with the Wirral peninsula forming the spout and the narrow stretch between Lancashire, Yorkshire and Derbyshire acting as the handle. All of the Wirral was in Cheshire as were some of the southern suburbs of Manchester, but Warrington and Widnes became part of the county after the local government changes came into effect in 1974. In this book, references are made to places and railways outside Cheshire, especially in the Manchester area, because it is difficult to avoid but also because it helps to explain why certain railways took the course that they did within Cheshire. Take as an example the CLC line between Skelton Junction, north of Altrincham, and Brinnington Junction, east of Stockport; travelling eastwards the journey takes us out of Cheshire at Baguley, returning to the county at Northenden Junction but leaving once again near Cheadle Junction before entering Cheshire again east of Stockport Tiviot Dale. If we consider the MS&LR Sheffield route, this first enters Cheshire east of Guide Bridge before entering Derbyshire beyond Broadbottom. The line then runs along the Cheshire/Derbyshire border before, surprisingly, returning to Cheshire at the entrance to Woodhead Tunnel. Indeed, the first part of the tunnel lay within the county.

The reference to the Sheffield route via Woodhead is a reminder of the contrasts in railway journeys within Cheshire. Not surprisingly, the routes that headed east into the Pennines were more steeply graded and incorporated heavier engineering works than lines on the Cheshire plain, although rivers and their valleys were bridged in several places around the county. On the Woodhead route, for instance, gradients were as steep as 1 in 77 east of Guide Bridge and the continuous climb of 14 miles from there to the tunnel featured gradients in the range of 1 in 100 to 1 in 122 for several miles. Another challenging climb was the last Midland route from Manchester to Derby via Cheadle Heath and Hazel Grove, featuring gradients of, for the most part, between 1 in 100 and 1 in 140 in Cheshire, together with the passage through Disley Tunnel, the longest wholly in Cheshire. Elsewhere in the county gradients were a little easier on the major routes. The Manchester–London route to Crewe has nothing steeper than 1 in 240 with much of the route flatter than 1 in 500. Along the West Coast Main Line the gradients are mainly easier than 1 in 300.

Another feature of Cheshire's railways is the viaduct. The rivers that cross from the hills in the east to the estuaries in the west, have caused railway engineers to build viaducts. These straddle the rivers Weaver, Dane and Bollin on more than one railway line while the two largest watercourses, the Mersey and the Dee, have acted as boundary lines as well as forcing the hands of early engineers. The Mersey is arguably responsible for the most spectacular example of civil engineering in the county – the splendid viaduct at the north end of Stockport. If you think the railway viaduct at Runcorn is more impressive then that, too, crosses the Mersey.

Within Cheshire there are no large cities – Birkenhead, Stockport and Chester were the biggest towns in the county before the boundary changes of 1973 – and much of the county was, and indeed still is, rural. As mentioned earlier, the reason for the variety of railway lines and locomotives has much to do with the commercial force of the two large cities lying just beyond the boundaries of Cheshire – Liverpool and Manchester. Coincidentally, it was the southerly extension from the historic railway between these two commercial giants that gave Cheshire its first railway, one of the oldest trunk routes in Britain (or the world for that matter).

The original network in Cheshire of three lines from Warrington, Chester and Manchester that joined at Crewe passed into the ownership of the London & North Western Railway in 1846 and that company set about guarding its territory aggressively. It managed to reduce the North Staffordshire Railway's designs on Manchester business to traffic arrangements that mainly favoured the larger company. It also resisted the GWR's attempts to penetrate Liverpool and Manchester but the GWR did succeed in reaching Merseyside via the Birkenhead line, operated jointly with the LNWR between that town and Chester. The same arrangement with the LNWR saw through GWR services to Manchester.

The LNWR suffered greater and more sustained competition from the MS&LR, who, as the former Sheffield, Ashton-under-Lyne & Manchester Railway, had already acquired access to Manchester in 1841, prior to the existence of the LNWR. Under the guidance of Edward Watkin, a former employee of the LNWR, the MS&LR set about forming alliances in order to challenge the LNWR's grip on railway business in the area. The most significant move was the support by the MS&LR and Great Northern Railway of a group of schemes across north Cheshire that would become the CLC in 1867. By 1866 the result was a line from Godley Junction, where there was a connection with the MS&LR's Sheffield route, to Stockport, Altrincham and

Northwich. Once the line from Northwich to Helsby had been added in 1869, the CLC was able to gain access to the Wirral and the docks on the Cheshire side of the Mersey. Although outside Cheshire, it is worth adding that the crucial blow to the LNWR came when authorisation was given to the MS&LR to build a line from Cornbrook, on the Manchester South Junction & Altrincham Railway (MSJ&AR), to Cressington on the Garston & Liverpool Railway. The line, which opened in 1873, had been supported by the GNR and the Midland Railway.

The Midland gained access to Manchester via Marple and Hyde Junction, once the route from Derby had been completed in 1867, but a more direct route was found when the MS&LR and Midland Joint line between Romiley and Ashbury Junction opened in 1875. Congestion at London Road forced the Midland to look for better access into the city and this led to their building another line, this time from Throstle Nest East Junction to Heaton Mersey Junction. Opening in 1880, it gave the Midland Railway an access to the new CLC station at Manchester Central via Bredbury Junction, Tiviot Dale and Heaton Mersey. Even that was not the end of the Midland's attempts to improve its access into Manchester. In 1902 its express trains used a newly constructed line from New Mills South Junction to Cheadle Heath. Meanwhile, as the third member of the CLC, it gained access across Cheshire to the industrial complex at Northwich and, beyond, to Chester. The MS&LR went further by opening a line west from Chester to Hawarden Bridge and then south to Wrexham in 1890. They followed this with a joint project that resulted in a line running north through the Wirral to Bidston in 1896.

From these efforts by different railway companies to reach Manchester and Liverpool it may be seen how there came to be such a variety of motive power in Cheshire until the end of the 1950s. The CLC never owned its own locomotives; they used those of the companies forming the committee, namely the MS&LR (later the Great Central Railway), the Midland and, to a lesser extent, the GNR. The NSR lost its remaining locomotives during the LMS era but other examples of pre-grouping types could be seen in the county well into BR days.

There were eleven sheds, excluding sub-sheds, at the dawn of the nationalised network. Crewe, Chester and the Birkenhead area accounted for more than half of these with Crewe North and South, Chester's GWR and LMS sheds, as well as its CLC depot, and Birkenhead and Bidston sheds, supplemented by those at Stockport, Northwich, Macclesfield and Alsager. Much of the locomotive stock by this time was, of course, of LMS origin, together with several different types of GWR and LNER locomotives. Of particular interest was the variety of pre-grouping classes represented within the county. For reasons that will be clear, given the historical perspective, Cheshire was home to engines from the LNWR, Midland, MS&LR, GCR and GWR companies. It is difficult, however, to explain the existence of other locomotives from the Lancashire & Yorkshire Railway (L&YR), North London Railway (NLR), North Eastern Railway (NER) and Great Eastern Railway (GER) at work within the county. Perhaps, the most unusual allocation was that of two Caledonian Railway 0–4–0 shunters at Crewe.

At various times during the 1950s there were more than sixty different classes of locomotives based at Cheshire's eleven sheds, but many more could be seen on a regular basis at work in the county. For instance, until electrification of the Woodhead route, Gresley A3 Pacifics and V2 2–6–2s appeared routinely, along with B1 and B17 4–6–0s, O1 and O4 2–8–0s, K3 2–6–0s and various pre-grouping types that disappeared before or soon after the beginning of the nationalised era. Then there was the Summer Saturday traffic, often featuring motive power not based in Cheshire, which would bring a procession of trains from the Midlands and Eastern England through Cheshire to Blackpool and Southport.

During the 1950s most of the pre-grouping stock disappeared so that by 1960 much of what was left of the older classes was either of Midland or LNWR origin. The first sheds in the BR era to close to steam did so in that year, the casualties being the GWR and CLC depots at Chester. In 1962 the only NSR motive power depot in the county (at Alsager) shut its doors for the last time while the following year saw the closure of the last GCR shed in Cheshire (at Bidston). When

Crewe North closed in 1965 it marked the end of the era of express passenger haulage along the WCML by Cheshire-based locomotives and three years later, in May 1968, Stockport became the last steam shed to close in Cheshire, a mere three months before the curtain came down on the steam era.

Although preserved steam locomotives can still be seen in the county, the steam era that many of us remember passed into history forty years ago. At this point, therefore, it seems appropriate to look at some of the images of that era and explore the different aspects of steam in Cheshire in more detail but, before doing so, I would like to acknowledge the vital contribution made by many photographers. David Chatfield, Peter Fitton, Doug Darby, John Hilton, Tom Heavyside and Ron Gee have all made a significant number of photographs available as well as providing additional help. In addition, I am very grateful to Richard Casserley, Tony Oldfield, Doug Rendell, Gavin Morrison, A.C. Gilbert and A.S. Darby for their help and I acknowledge with thanks the contributions from various collections including Photos from the Fifties, Transport Treasury, RAS Marketing, The Stephenson Locomotive Society, the Kidderminster Railway Museum Trust, Paul Chancellor and Andrew Ingram.

My wife, Joyce, and daughter, Helen, have been very accommodating in allowing me the space to store a significant amount of research material including books, magazines and maps and I thank them both very much.

A number of railway companies are mentioned in the text on more than a few occasions and I have, therefore, taken the liberty of referring to them by their initials. For the benefit of those readers not familiar with these initials, I list below the full names together with their abbreviated titles for ease of reference.

BL&CJR	Birkenhead, Lancashire & Cheshire Junction Railway
BR	British Railways (later British Rail)
CLC	Cheshire Lines Committee
GCR	Great Central Railway
GER	Great Eastern Railway
GJR	Grand Junction Railway
GNR	Great Northern Railway
GWR	Great Western Railway
L&YR	Lancashire & Yorkshire Railway
LMSR	London Midland & Scottish Railway (often referred to as LMS)
LNER	London & North Eastern Railway
LNWR	London & North Western Railway
MS&LR	Manchester, Sheffield & Lincolnshire Railway
MSJ&AR	Manchester South Junction & Altrincham Railway
NER	North Eastern Railway
NLR	North London Railway
NSR	North Staffordshire Railway
SA&MR	Sheffield, Ashton-under-Lyne and Manchester Railway
WCML	West Coast Main Line

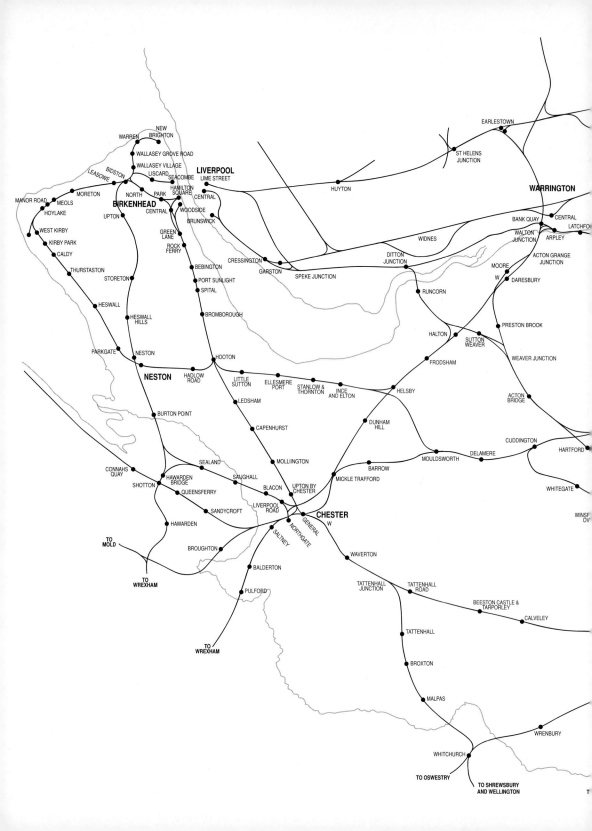

1

The West Coast Main Line

Cheshire's first railway opened on 4 July 1837 and it was a very significant railway. The GJR's route from Warrington to Birmingham was the first major extension southwards from the formative Liverpool & Manchester Railway, following the initial short branch from Newton Junction (now Earlestown) to Warrington. It was built in the reign of William IV and mention of its engineers only adds to its historical significance. Joseph Locke and George Stephenson were in charge of construction but, owing to disagreements, Stephenson withdrew his involvement and Locke was left in sole charge. He would later take responsibility for other sections (most notably through the fells) of what would become known as the West Coast Main Line.

The steepest section along the route through Cheshire is the 1 in 135 near Acton Grange, where the railway crosses over the Manchester Ship Canal, but the bigger challenge for steam traction was the southbound start from Crewe. This involved a climb of 10 miles to Whitmore in Staffordshire, including over 3 miles at 1 in 177 south of Betley Road. It was on a special northbound run, down the gradient to Crewe, that the streamlined Stanier Pacific, no. 6220 *Coronation*, broke the British speed record for steam on 29 June 1937 at 114mph. It was a run that almost ended in disaster when it entered Crewe too fast, through a series of crossovers. Thankfully, it managed to remain upright but the record it claimed was held for just over a year before *Mallard* took the honour in 1938. The line is also associated with the legendary run of *Hardwicke* in 1895 during the 'Races to the North', a series of competing runs between West Coast and East Coast trains. 'Hardwicke', a 2–4–0 of modest proportions, averaged 67.2mph between Crewe and Carlisle, a remarkable feat for the time.

The engineering features in Cheshire include the twenty arches of the Dutton viaduct over the River Weaver (north of Acton Bridge), the Weaver Junction flyover (believed to be the first of its kind in the world) that carries the up line from Liverpool over the main line, and the burrowing freight lines at Crewe that allowed goods traffic to pass under the main line without interfering with passenger services. The features at Weaver Junction and at Crewe were products of LNWR thinking, many years after the railway opened, and were designed to reduce congestion on their principal route. Weaver Junction is at the southern end of an 8½-mile branch that connects the WCML to Ditton Junction, near Widnes. Completed in 1869 it allowed trains between Liverpool and the south to avoid Earlestown and Warrington. At the northern end of this connecting line stands another major engineering feature, the Runcorn Bridge that crosses the Mersey. Of the junctions along the Cheshire section of the WCML the last connection was made when the Over & Wharton branch opened in 1882 but this last-named branch near Winsford closed in 1982, long after passenger services had ceased.

Before the grouping of 1923 there were eight stations, including Crewe, along the WCML in Cheshire. To the south of Crewe, Betley Road closed to passengers in 1945. To the north, Minshull Vernon closed in 1942 while Winsford, Hartford and Acton Bridge have all survived. Two more casualties of the 1940s were Preston Brook in 1948 and Moore (near to one of the two sets of water troughs in the county) in 1943. On the Liverpool branch in Cheshire, Sutton Weaver closed as long ago as 1931 while Runcorn serves a growing catchment area.

Following the initial extension from the historic Liverpool & Manchester Railway to Warrington, the West Coast Main Line was built southwards to Birmingham by the Grand Junction Railway and completed in 1837. We shall follow the route south through Cheshire beginning with this view of a Preston-based Stanier 'Jubilee', no. 45633 *Aden*, on a down relief Euston–Workington train approaching Acton Grange Junction on 18 May 1959. The train is on a rising gradient of 1 in 135 leading towards the viaduct over the Manchester Ship Canal. *(M.H.Walshaw/Photos from The Fifties)*

At the dawn of the BR era, an unrebuilt 'Royal Scot', no. 6110 *Grenadier Guardsman*, still in LMS livery, is seen at Moore Troughs, having just passed through the disused Moore station, faintly visible to the rear of the train. The locomotive, based at Carlisle Upperby, is in charge of a southbound parcels train on 15 May 1948. *(J.D.Darby)*

A BR 'Clan' 4-6-2, no. 72009 *Clan Stewart*, is in charge of the 6.20 a.m. Carlisle–Crewe stopping train about to pass under the Birkenhead Joint line near Daresbury on 31 August 1963. From Carlisle the train has taken no less than 4½ hours to reach this location. *(Peter Fitton)*

A 'Princess Coronation', no. 46225 *Duchess of Gloucester*, is seen in the cutting at Dutton with a Perth–Euston express on 31 August 1963. It is approaching Weaver Junction, where the lines from Liverpool join the main line. *(Peter Fitton)*

Before continuing south from Weaver Junction, it is worth taking a look at the Liverpool branch of the main line. When the Grand Junction Railway opened the main line to Birmingham, all trains from Liverpool travelled via the Liverpool & Manchester route as far as Newton Junction (later Earlestown) and then south through Warrington. In 1869 the LNWR opened a shorter route to Liverpool which also helped to reduce congestion on the West Coast Main Line, north of Weaver Junction. A 'Princess Royal' 4–6–2, no. 46207 *Princess Arthur of Connaught,* has just crossed the Runcorn Bridge with a seventeen-coach 'Merseyside Express' (10 a.m. ex-Liverpool Lime Street) on 8 August 1959. *(M.H.Walshaw / Photos from The Fifties)*

At Runcorn station a 'Silver Jubilee', no. 45629 *Straits Settlements*, departs with a Liverpool Lime Street service on 26 March 1961. The station was undergoing reconstruction at the time as part of the electrification of the Liverpool branch. The sign to the right of the locomotive refers to the works taking place while beyond the sign a freight-only branch drops down to the nearby chemical works. *(David Chatfield)*

A Shrewsbury-based Standard class 5 4–6–0, no. 73096, approaches Runcorn at the head of the 8.45 a.m. Plymouth–Liverpool Lime Street on 15 July 1961. Although the masts and wires had been erected, electric services to and from Liverpool would not commence until June 1962. *(Michael Mensing)*

A Stanier 'Princess Coronation', no. 46233 *Duchess of Sutherland*, is seen under the wires at Aston Heath, near Weaver Junction, with a Euston–Liverpool Lime Street relief train on 31 August 1963. Electric services had commenced in the previous year between Liverpool and Crewe. The locomotive was based at Edge Hill depot in Liverpool at the time and, though withdrawn early in the following year, it was subsequently preserved. *(Peter Fitton)*

The 12.50 p.m. Saturdays-only Liverpool Lime Street–Crewe stopping train is a lightweight assignment for 'Silver Jubilee', no. 45733 *Novelty*, at Weaver Junction on 16 September 1961. *(John Hilton)*

A smartly turned out 'Royal Scot' 4-6-0, no. 46146 *The Rifle Brigade*, is in charge of an up express south of Weaver Junction in the early evening of 12 April 1953. *(J.D. Darby)*

Apart from Crewe, there were only three stations on the West Coast Main Line in Cheshire at the end of the steam era. These stations – Winsford, Hartford and Acton Bridge – remain open today. The next sequence of pictures focuses on Acton Bridge in the period immediately before electrification. In this view from the signal box, a 'Princess Coronation', no. 46245 *City of London*, at the head of the Glasgow–Euston 'Royal Scot' express, awaits the right away on 9 July 1960. The station's busy goods yard was part of the daily scene at this time, before the Beeching era. *(John Hilton)*

The 8.22 a.m. push-pull service to Warrington and St Helens Shaw Street, with Ivatt 2–6–2 tank no. 41289, at the front end, is about to depart Acton Bridge station on 29 March 1960. The locomotive was based at Sutton Oak shed in St Helens. *(John Hilton)*

It is midsummer in Cheshire and the crew of an unidentified rebuilt 'Patriot' await further instructions from the signal box at Acton Bridge. Their train, the 'Empress Voyager', ran nortbound on Tuesdays in order to connect with Canadian Pacific sailings from Liverpool. A southbound train has been signalled while a freight train is held in the down loop in June 1960. *(John Hilton)*

Along much of the West Coast Main Line in England, the LNWR 0–8–0s, designed by Bowen-Cooke, could be seen on freight duties. On 15 August 1960 a G2 example of this class, no. 49447, leaves the down loop with the 2.45 p.m. Northwich–Bamfurlong freight. The engine, which was based at Wigan's Springs Branch shed, would have traversed the CLC route from Northwich and joined the main line at Hartford Junction. *(John Hilton)*

About 2 miles south of Acton Bridge, the unique BR Pacific, no. 71000 *Duke of Gloucester*, passes Hartford Junction with the 10.10 a.m. Glasgow–Birmingham express on 1 June 1960. The two tracks beyond the locomotive connect the West Coast Main Line with the CLC Chester-Manchester route and were used, primarily, by freight trains such as that hauled by the 0–8–0 in the previous picture. *(John Hilton)*

At Hartford station an unrebuilt 'Patriot' 4–6–0, no. 45524 *Blackpool*, approaches with the 12.05 p.m. Euston–Workington on 21 June 1951. (*T.G. Wassell/Photos from the Fifties*)

North of Winsford station, a short branch veered off to the west. It supported a passenger service once but the terminus at Over & Wharton, the only station on the line, closed a long time ago. The line was used from time to time for storing engines awaiting the breaker's yard and in this picture, taken on 21 February 1959, the line-up of derelict locomotives includes former London, Tilbury & Southend Railway tank engines including no. 41948 of the 4–4–2 types and no. 41984 of the 0–6–2 variety. LNWR 0–8–0s make up the balance of the line up, all awaiting the call to Crewe Works for scrapping. (*David Chatfield*)

Shortly before the inauguration of electric services between Liverpool and Crewe, a Chester-based BR Standard class 4 4–6–0, no. 75035, approaches Winsford station with the 1.45 p.m. Crewe–Garston freight on 1 June 1962. *(John Hilton)*

A northbound express with a rebuilt 'Patriot', no. 45531 *Sir Frederick Harrison*, from Edge Hill, Liverpool, at the helm is seen near Minshull Vernon on 28 June 1953. The station at Minshull Vernon closed in 1942. *(J.D. Darby)*

At the north end of Crewe station, a Blackpool-based 'Silver Jubilee' 4–6–0, no. 45571 *South Africa*, waits for departure with the 12.15 p.m. London Euston–Blackpool Central on 26 November 1960. To the left, another 'Jubilee' 4–6–0 waits for its next duty while English Electric D216 stands at the head of another northbound train on the right. *(Michael Mensing)*

In this pre-war photograph at Crewe, streamlined 'Princess Coronation', no. 6220 *Coronation*, at the head of the 'Coronation Scot', evokes memories of the record-breaking run of 1937 when, in the course of taking the speed record for steam, it approached the station at too high a speed and had to negotiate a series of crossovers outside Crewe station at over 50mph. Fortunately, the engine managed to remain upright and disaster was averted. The train is seen here on 2 September 1938. *(J.D.Darby)*

The 10.30 a.m. London Euston–Liverpool Lime Street is about 3 miles south of Crewe and approaching Basford Hall sidings with an LMS 2P 4–4–0, no. 40655 (of Crewe North), piloting 'Silver Jubilee' 4–6–0, no. 45582 *Central Provinces*, in charge on 4 April 1958. *(Michael Mensing)*

Earlier, we saw 'Royal Scots' in original condition and in rebuilt form. Here we see a rebuilt 'Scot' prior to fitting with smoke deflectors. No. 6103 *Royal Scots Fusilier*, in LMS livery, passes under bridge 71 with a mixed freight on 19 April 1946. The engine is from Leeds Holbeck but, judging from its condition, it is possibly running-in after overhaul at Crewe. *(J.D. Darby)*

Another southbound train passes under bridge 71 and this time it is the Glasgow–Euston 'Royal Scot' express with 'Princess Coronation', no. 46256 *Sir William A. Stanier*, in charge as it climbs the bank towards Whitmore on 11 October 1955. *(J.D. Darby)*

Edge Hill locomotive, 'Silver Jubilee' 4–6–0, no. 45681 *Aboukir*, passes the site of Betley Road station, close to Cheshire's southern boundary, with a Liverpool–Euston express on Sunday 25 May 1952. The locomotive is hauling fifteen coaches up the 1 in 177 towards Whitmore. *(J.D. Darby)*

2

West Cheshire

Of the four railways that meet the WCML at Crewe, the first and the last in chronological order, head into west Cheshire. The Chester & Crewe Railway became part of the GJR on 1 July 1840, shortly before the line opened to Chester, while the LNWR route to Shrewsbury opened in 1858. From the Chester line the LNWR built a branch from Tattenhall Junction to Whitchurch, on the Shrewsbury route. Opening in 1872 it appears to have had a tactical purpose in attempting to draw traffic away from the GWR's main line between Shrewsbury and Chester but, if this was the case, then it did not succeed. Receipts were poor and the line lost its passenger service in 1957 with closure following in 1963. From the Shrewsbury line, a branch was built south of Nantwich to Market Drayton in Shropshire. It opened in 1863 and, four years later, was connected to the separate Wellington & Drayton Railway. Absorbed by the Great Western in 1897, this line saw through-running to Crewe from Wellington by GWR locomotives until passenger services ceased in 1963. Closure came in 1967.

The GWR's principal route into Cheshire was via the Shrewsbury & Chester Railway's line that opened throughout in 1848. A protracted battle followed between the GWR and the LNWR over access into Chester and this was only resolved by Parliament in 1854 to the GWR's advantage. The GWR eventually gained access to the commercial hub of Merseyside by jointly (with the LNWR) taking possession in 1860 of the Chester–Birkenhead route that had opened twenty years earlier. In the following year express trains ran from Paddington to Birkenhead. The combined forces of the GWR and LNWR proceeded to open up the Wirral with connections from their main line. In 1863 they opened a branch from Hooton eastwards to Helsby, on the Chester–Warrington route. In 1866 a further branch was opened from Hooton heading west to Parkgate by the Dee Estuary. In 1886 this line was extended northwards to West Kirby, where a new station was built adjacent to that serving Birkenhead trains.

At the northern tip of the Wirral, railway projects saw Hoylake connected to Birkenhead in 1866 and to West Kirby in 1878. Wallasey and New Brighton were connected by rail to Birkenhead from 1888 and Seacombe followed suit in 1895. With the completion of the Mersey tunnel in 1886 the Wirral benefited from direct rail services into Liverpool and this marked a new phase in the development of the Wirral as a commuter belt for the city. The problems caused by smoke in the tunnels led to the electrification of these routes into Liverpool in 1903.

The final entrant into the Wirral was, surprisingly, the MS&LR. However, it had already gained access to Chester through its membership of the CLC, and an opportunity now arose to take advantage of potential traffic in North Wales. Its line from Chester Northgate opened to Wrexham in 1890 and then, with the Wrexham, Mold & Connah's Quay Railway, it resurrected an earlier scheme to open a line between Birkenhead and North Wales. This opened to passengers in 1896 but hopes of gaining access to Liverpool via the Mersey Tunnel were dashed by the Mersey Railway. So, an alternative terminus was found at Seacombe. This railway was later absorbed by the GCR and when that company became part of the LNER at the grouping, LNER locomotive types found themselves working in this westerly outpost of Cheshire.

The first junction to be formed at Crewe was with the Chester line in 1840 and a 9F 2–10–0 is seen on this line with a passenger train. A former Franco-Crosti-boilered 9F 2–10–0 at the head of such a train is an unusual sight but no. 92026 is hauling a railtour special to Crewe while passing Beeston & Tarporley on 26 February 1967. *(Peter Fitton)*

Crewe was one of the few places along the WCML where GWR locos could be seen regularly. Typical workings included the Wellington–Crewe passenger services and freights. The town's Gresty Lane shed, a sub-shed of Wellington situated along the Shrewsbury line, acted as a stabling point for such locomotives. This view shows Ivatt class 2 2–6–2 tank, no. 41201, in the company of GWR locomotives on 12 May 1963, one month before the shed closed. Behind the tank engine is a 'Hall', no. 6903 *Belmont Hall*, and a 'Grange', no. 6821 *Leaton Grange*. The skeleton frame of the roof appears to be serving little purpose apart from, possibly, stabilising the shed walls. Above the shed, on the left, is the Shrewsbury line. *(Peter Fitton)*

A GWR Prairie tank engine, no. 4158, passes Gresty Lane with the 5.10 p.m. Crewe–Wellington service, calling at all stations on 12 May 1958. The locomotive was based at Wellington depot. *(J.D. Darby)*

Another Wellington-based locomotive, GWR 0–6–0 pannier tank, no. 3732, heads for Crewe with a pick-up freight between Nantwich and Willaston on 25 February 1961. *(David Chatfield)*

An Ivatt 2–6–2 tank, no. 41232, approaches Nantwich with a Crewe–Wellington service on 25 Februar
1961. Beyond this town the train will branch away from the Shrewsbury line and follow the route t
Market Drayton and Wellington. *(David Chatfield)*

The GWR's main access into Cheshire was via its Shrewsbury–Chester route. At Saltney Junction th
GWR lines meet those from Holyhead and run side-by-side to Chester. In this picture, a GWR 2–6–0
no. 7313, has just crossed the River Dee with what is almost certainly a train from Pwllheli an
Barmouth on 13 June 1959. *(David Chatfield)*

In this undated view at the same location as the previous picture, a Stanier 'Jubilee' 4–6–0, no. 45726 *Vindictive*, at the head of a parcels train, passes the gas works on the approach to Chester from the North Wales main line. *(David Chatfield)*

Taken from the City Walls, this view shows a GWR 0–6–2 tank engine, no. 6694, of Croes Newydd shed, Wrexham, at the head of a passenger train and leaving Chester behind on 13 June 1959. This is the only point where the railway passes briefly within the walled area of Chester near to the corner occupied by the Water Tower. *(David Chatfield)*

A Hughes 2–6–0 'Crab', no. 42727, is seen on an SLS Special to North Wales having curved round from Chester General station on 27 March 1966. The lines curving away to the left form a triangle with the Birkenhead line that passes in front of the former GWR motive power depot in the background. *(Peter Fitton)*

Chester-based Midland Compound, no. 41107, under a fine array of signals, arrives at its home town with an express from North Wales in July 1951. To the right of the engine is the GWR motive power depot. *(RAS Marketing)*

A GWR 'Hall', no. 6926 *Holkham Hall*, rests at the buffer stops in Chester General station after arriving from the Midlands on 14 March 1959. *(David Chatfield)*

While in Chester it is well worth a trip across the city to the small terminus at Northgate. Motive power here in the early 1950s was of mainly GCR origin; locomotive types such as N5 0–6–2 tank, no. 69281, here at Chester Northgate station with the 5.12 p.m. Chester–Wrexham service on 6 June 1956. This particular class dates from the GCR's predecessor, the MS&LR. The signals show that the train will cross from right to left before veering westwards across the bottom of the Wirral and then heading south through Shotton and into North Wales. *(Ron Gee)*

The journey around West Cheshire now continues with a look at activities on the Wirral. Approaching Chester from the Wirral is BR class 9 2–10–0, no. 92163, on an Up steel train passing Chester no. 4 box on 5 January 1967. The former GWR motive power depot that closed in 1960 had been converted to a diesel depot by this time. *(Peter Fitton)*

A Stanier 2–6–4 tank, no. 42587, leaves Ledsham with the last 3.25 p.m. Birkenhead–Paddington express on 5 March 1967. At Chester the train would reverse and continue behind a 'Jubilee' or Stanier class 5 4–6–0 instead of GWR motive power which had been scrapped by this time. *(Peter Fitton)*

The main junction between Chester and Birkenhead is at Hooton where there is a branch to Ellesmere Port and Helsby, on the Chester–Warrington line. There was a further branch to the west to Parkgate and West Kirby. All these lines were jointly owned by the GWR and LNWR. In this undated picture, a Stanier class 4 2–6–4 tank, no. 42568, of Chester shed, arrives with a Western Region express from Birkenhead. *(David Lawrence/Photos from the Fifties)*

In the industrial part of the Wirral, a grimy Stanier class 5 4–6–0, no. 44761, moves empty coaching stock through Rock Ferry station on a cold 5 January 1967. Travellers to and from Liverpool were required to change at Rock Ferry which was then the limit for electric services. *(Peter Fitton)*

In this view from Rock Ferry station, in the southern suburbs of Birkenhead, we see a BR standard class 9 2–10–0, no. 92048, with bogie bolsters heading in the direction of Chester on a frosty 5 January 1967. *(Peter Fitton)*

Within the dark and gloomy confines of Birkenhead Woodside station, a beam of light illuminates GWR Prairie tank engine, no. 4125, awaiting departure with the 1.43 p.m. all stations to Chester on 20 April 1954. *(H.C. Casserley)*

Birkenhead Woodside looks ominously bare except for the railtour special train headed by a Hughes 'Crab' 2–6–0, no. 42942, as it prepares to depart. *(GNSRA/Forrest/www.transporttreasury.co.uk)*

One of the Birkenhead-based GWR 2–6–2 tank engines, no. 4129, rests between duties at its home depot on 20 April 1954. Despite the date, it still retains its GWR identity. *(H.C. Casserley)*

The coal and ash plants at Birkenhead motive power depot dominate their surroundings, including two BR Standard class 9 2–10–0s, nos 92160 and 92089, and Stanier 2–8–0, no. 48676, on 28 June 1966. *(Tom Heavyside)*

When this photograph was taken on 24 February 1959, two of this small class of ten Fowler 0–6–0 'Dock Tanks' were based at Birkenhead shed. Here is no. 47164 at its home depot with one of the numerous Fowler 0–6–0 tank engines shunting in the background. The 'Dock Tanks' were short wheelbase engines designed for working on tight curves. *(Peter Fitton)*

Another class of ten shunting locomotives was active in Birkenhead. Designed for the LMSR by Kitson in 1932, a further batch of these 0–4–0 saddle tanks was built in 1953 including no. 47006. It was only three years old when photographed at Birkenhead Docks on 29 March 1956. *(David Chatfield)*

While several of the north Wirral towns were served by electric trains, Seacombe, to the north of Birkenhead, was overlooked. Instead, it served as a terminus for trains to Wrexham Exchange and Wrexham Central via Heswall and Neston. On 16 May 1959, a BR class 3 2–6–2 tank, no. 82020, departs with the 12.45 p.m. for Wrexham. *(M.H. Walshaw/Photos from the Fifties)*

Eleven minutes after the departure of the Wrexham service, another train arrives at the terminus, hauled by an Ivatt class 2 2–6–2 tank, no. 41231, with the 11.25 a.m. from Wrexham. The locomotives working the Seacombe trains were based at Wrexham Rhosddu shed that closed in 1960. *(M.H. Walshaw/Photos from the Fifties)*

At Bidston station the Wrexham line branches away from the Hoylake and West Kirby line. The BR class 3 2–6–2 tank, no. 82020, seen earlier at Seacombe, is about to depart from Bidston with the 2.40 p.m. service from Wrexham on 19 September 1959. Wrexham is still served by trains from the Wirral but from Bidston instead of Seacombe, which lost its passenger service at the beginning of 1960. (*H.C. Casserley*)

The first significant closure in this part of Cheshire was the decidedly rural branch line from West Kirby to Hooton. The last passenger train ran on 15 September 1956 and after complete closure of the line in 1962, the course of the railway became the linear Wirral Country Park. In this undated view, GWR 2–6–2 tank, no. 4126, of Birkenhead shed, awaits departure from West Kirby. (*David Lawrence/ Photos from the Fifties*)

Another view of West Kirby station shows GWR 2–6–2, tank no. 4126, with a train for Hooton. Behind the train, the signal-box marks the junction with the electric line from Liverpool and Birkenhead that uses an adjacent terminus. *(David Lawrence/Photos from the Fifties)*

Apart from their use on West Kirby trains, the GWR 2–6–2 tank engines were employed on the Helsby services via Hooton. No. 4124 is seen at Helsby awaiting departure with a Birkenhead train on 27 June 1956. The footbridge above the rear coach also serves trains on the Chester–Warrington line, to the right and out of view. *(David Chatfield)*

3

From Chester to Manchester

In 1850, when the Birkenhead, Lancashire & Cheshire Junction Railway (BL&CJR) opened their route from Chester to Walton Junction, on the south side of Warrington, Chester consolidated its status as an important railway centre, with, at that time, lines from five different directions converging on the city.

The BL&CJR's original proposals had been more ambitious but its proposed route from Hooton, on the Wirral, to Heaton Mersey, north of Stockport, was opposed by the persuasive powers of the GJR, then in its final days before becoming a part of the newly formed LNWR. Initially, there were two stations, at Frodsham and Dunham, on their revised route, but Runcorn (the first Runcorn station) and Norton were added in 1851 and Helsby in 1852. The BL&CJR later became the Birkenhead Railway which, in turn, came under the joint control of the LNWR and GWR. As a result the GWR gained a small foothold in Manchester and, prior to nationalisation, its motive power such as 'Halls' and 'Saints' could be seen regularly at Manchester Exchange.

The second route between Chester and Manchester came about in a more piecemeal manner, almost as an afterthought. Its origins lay in the ambitions of both the GNR and the MS&LR to challenge the LNWR's near monopoly on rail-borne traffic in the area. The completion of this route has much to do with the drive and ambition of one man, the MS&LR's chairman, Edward Watkin. It was his support of four schemes, the Stockport & Woodley Junction Railway, the Cheshire Midland Railway, the West Cheshire Railway and the Stockport, Timperley & Altrincham Junction Railway that led to the first strands of what would become the Cheshire Lines Committee coming together in 1863.

The Cheshire Midland's scheme was the more significant at the time as it ran from the southern terminus of the Manchester South Junction & Altrincham Railway (MSJ&AR) resulting in a continuous line from Manchester to the salt producing area of Northwich. The MSJ&AR had opened their line from Manchester Oxford Road to Altrincham in 1849, primarily for passenger traffic. It is likely that this southern extension would have led to the authorisation of the West Cheshire Railway Act in 1861 for the construction of a line from Northwich to Helsby. This was intended to make a connection with the Birkenhead Joint route at Helsby from Hooton. The new line, which opened in 1869 to goods and in the following year to passengers, gave access to the industrial base at Birkenhead. Branches were opened from Cuddington to Winsford and Over (primarily for the transport of salt) and also to Winnington in 1870, where the freight-only line served the growing chemical industry.

There appeared to be no hurry to extend the line from Mouldsworth to Chester and it was the Chester & West Cheshire Junction Railway, formed in 1865, who were authorised to build a line into the city. It opened in 1874 with a new station at Chester Northgate but, in fact, it was the CLC, given full legal status in 1867, who built the line. At the time the Committee was an equal partnership between three companies: the MS&LR, the GNR and the Midland Railway (MR). At the grouping in 1923 the CLC, surprisingly, retained its independence and passed to the LNER and LMS in the ratio of two to one, accounting for the presence of LNER locomotives on trains in this area until the mid-1950s.

It is worth mentioning that the CLC line between the two cities has also fulfilled, in part, the role of a diversionary route for Manchester–London expresses. This was due to an LNWR branch that opened between Sandbach and Northwich in 1867. During the LNWR era through-coaches ran between Oxford Road and Euston while in the early stages of WCML electrification, affecting the Manchester–Crewe lines, there was extensive use made of the CLC route and the Sandbach branch by long-distance trains.

In the last chapter we saw a GWR tank engine at Helsby with the footbridge over the rear coach of its train. The same footbridge can be seen above the Chester–Warrington tracks with BR class 5 4–6–0, no. 73144, about to depart in the Warrington direction on 1 August 1967. The lines leading to Ellesmere Port and Hooton can be seen crossing to the left. (*Tom Heavyside*)

Opposite, top: A 'Royal Scot' 4–6–0, no. 46148 *The Manchester Regiment*, passes through a rock cutting of red sandstone on the approach to Frodsham station with the 5.35 p.m. Manchester Exchange–Llandudno express on 25 April 1964. (*Peter Fitton*)

Opposite, bottom: A little further north from Frodsham, a BR class 5 4–6–0, no. 73158, and BR class 9 2–10–0, no. 92085, at the head of a Stanlow–Leeds oil train are held at Halton signal-box in 1966. (*Tony Oldfield*)

Having passed under the main line to Liverpool near Sutton Weaver, Warrington-bound trains cross over the West Coast Main Line at Norton, just south of Moore. With Runcorn's water tower in the background, a Stanier class 5 2–6–0, no. 42946, approaches the WCML with a Saturdays-only Rhyl–Manchester train on 31 August 1963. *(Peter Fitton)*

Crossing the West Coast Main Line in the opposite direction at 12.19 p.m. on the same day is an LNER B1 4–6–0, no. 61050, with the 10.10 a.m. Saturdays-only Sheffield–Bangor. *(Peter Fitton)*

In the previous chapter we caught a glimpse of Chester Northgate station with a Wrexham train about to leave. Whereas the Wrexham train cut across to the left on leaving the terminus, the Robinson D11 4–4–0, no. 62664 *Princess Mary*, at the head of a Manchester Central service on 6 June 1956, will curve round to the right. The Cheshire Line Committee had a long tradition of using MS&LR and GCR types on their network and the D11 was the last of these types to be used before all services were handled by LMS classes, shortly before the introduction of diesel multiple units. *(John Hilton)*

A Fowler 4–4–0, no. 40679, arrives at Chester Northgate with the 3.45 p.m. from Manchester Central on 6 June 1956. The Manchester line curves sharply in the distance to the right of the engine, while beyond the platform fence on the right, is the shed yard. In the sidings to the left is a push-pull set. *(Ron Gee)*

In this final look at Chester Northgate, a Fowler class 4 2–6–4 tank, no. 42319, waits with the next Manchester Central train on 13 June 1959. By this time all the GCR locos on the Chester services had moved away or been scrapped but diesel multiple units would soon replace steam on most trains. (*David Chatfield*)

Mickle Trafford station had closed when this picture was taken on 22 June 1952. The train is the 6.20 p.m. Sundays Manchester Central–Northgate with Stanier 2–6–4 tank, no. 42466, in charge. (*J.D. Darby*)

Cuddington, to the east of Delamere Forest, witnesses the passage of a Stanier class 5 4–6–0, no. 44822, in charge of a Mottram–Shotwick freight on 6 October 1961. (*John Hilton*)

West of Cuddington a branch line trailed south to Winsford & Over. Its purpose was primarily freight but, until 1931, there was a passenger service and an intermediate stop at Whitegate. A Fowler 4F 0–6–0, no. 44155, is seen at Whitegate with the 11.00 a.m. Winsford–Northwich goods on 21 February 1959. (*David Chatfield*)

A Warrington and District RCTS Rail Tour special has arrived at Winsford & Over station behind a GCR C13 4–4–2 tank, no. 67436, on 17 October 1953. The coaches appear to be old CLC non-corridor stock. This Chester Northgate engine was a regular on the Manchester–Chester service. *(T.G. Wassell/ Photos from the Fifties)*

Returning to Cuddington, the train about to depart on 8 August 1962 is a Chester–Northwich pick-up freight behind BR class 4 2–6–0, no.76089, of Trafford Park shed. *(John Hilton)*

Between Cuddington and Hartford & Greenbank stations the route crosses the West Coast Main Line. The 9.48 a.m. Manchester Central–Chester Northgate train, with Robinson D11 4–4–0, no. 62669 *Ypres*, in charge, is seen crossing the main line at Hartford on 26 September 1957. *(John Hilton)*

Another GCR type, Robinson O4/3 2–8–0, no. 63862, ambles through Hartford & Greenbank with an eastbound mineral train on 25 July 1961. This engine was one of many based at Gorton depot in Manchester. *(John Hilton)*

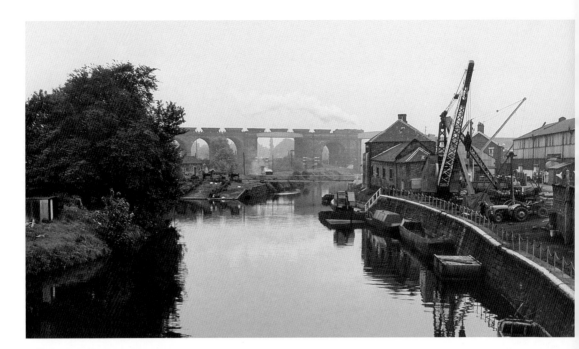

A Stanier 8F 2–8–0, at the head of ICI limestone wagons, crosses one of the most impressive engineering features on the former CLC railway network on 22 May 1963. It is crossing the two wrought iron girder bridges and the forty-eight arches of the viaduct spanning the Weaver Navigation and the River Dane, to the west of Northwich. *(David Chatfield)*

In this undated picture at Northwich station, a Crewe motor train is seen waiting for passengers. To the right, an ex-MS&LR J10 0–6–0, no. 65158, waits its next call of duty at Northwich shed. *(T. Noble/ David Chatfield Collection)*

Before continuing the journey towards Manchester, a brief trip will be made along the line to Sandbach. As well as supporting a passenger and freight service, it also acted as a diversionary route that proved its value when electrification of the Manchester–Crewe main line was taking place. At Whatcroft, between Northwich and Middlewich, a BR Britannia, no. 70031 *Byron*, of Longsight depot in Manchester, crosses the Trent & Mersey Canal with the southbound 'Pines Express' on 16 August 1960. *(John Hilton)*

Middlewich station is seen on a damp day as Ivatt class 2 2–6–2 tank engine, no. 41229, at the rear of its train, restarts the Northwich–Crewe push-pull service on 2 December 1959. *(David Chatfield)*

A Stanier class 5 2–6–0, no. 42956, based at Crewe South depot at the time, has left the Crewe–Manchester main line and, having passed the limit of the electrification gantries, is leaving Sandbach behind and making its way towards Northwich with a goods train on 29 July 1960. *(David Chatfield)*

Having travelled along the Sandbach–Northwich line, a 'Silver Jubilee' 4–6–0, no. 45709 *Implacable,* accelerates its diverted Birmingham–Manchester Piccadilly express away from Northwich on 3 March 1963. *(David Chatfield)*

For the railway enthusiast, no visit to Northwich was complete without a visit to the shed where, especially in the 1950s, there was plenty of variety. As well as the stud of Stanier 2–8–0s used on the limestone trains, there were various ex-GCR types including one of the largest allocations of ex-MS&LR J10 0–6–0s. The shed also housed two of the large Robinson L3 2–6–4 tank engines used for banking and trip freights around Hartford exchange sidings and along the branch to the ICI works at Winnington. This picture shows the remaining L3, no. 69052, on 7 July 1954, the year of its demise. (David Chatfield)

An unusual visitor to Northwich on 14 May 1960 is this WD 2–10–0, no. 90763, normally based at Carlisle Kingmoor, but returning from Bidston following a short trial period where it was used on John Summers iron ore trains. (David Chatfield)

Like the B1s, the LNER K3 2–6–0s were regular visitors to this line, but the one-coach evening mail to Manchester seems a lightweight load indeed for an engine of this size. No. 61853 is leaving Knutsford on 6 June 1962. By the end of that year all of this class would be withdrawn. *(David Chatfield)*

Opposite, top: A Thompson B1 4–6–0 of the LNER was not an uncommon sight on this route. In this picture no. 61269 was employed on the 7.37 a.m. Cuddington–Manchester commuter train. It is seen passing the chemical works between Lostock Gralam and Plumley on 1 March 1963. *(John Hilton)*

Opposite, bottom: A BR 'Britannia' 4–6–2, no. 70015 *Apollo*, passes Knutsford station on 14 May 1960 with the diverted 'Pines Express'. Because of electrification works, this Bournemouth train was booked to depart from Manchester Central instead of London Road. *(David Chatfield)*

Another LNER type seen in the area was the Gresley J39 0–6–0 such as no. 64717, of Gorton shed, which is seen passing under Parkgate Lane bridge, to the east of Knutsford, with a westbound goods. *(David Chatfield)*

Stanier 8F 2–8–0, no. 48667, presents a study of power as it is seen near Mobberley with a limestone train for ICI at Winnington on 11 September 1954. *(David Chatfield)*

The patience of the railway photographer was sometimes rewarded by something unusual and here is an interesting combination of 4–4–0s leaving Mobberley with the 1.40 p.m. Manchester Central–Chester Northgate on 12 November 1955. The leading engine is a GCR D11 4–4–0, no. 62664 *Princess Mary*, while the train engine is an LMS 4–4–0, no. 40675. *(David Chatfield)*

At the beginning of the BR era, a Stanier 8F 2–8–0, no. 8154, approaches with a limestone train on 3 April 1948 south of Ashley. This picture gives a good impression of the large size of these wagons. (*J.D. Darby*)

A GCR D6, no. 2101, leaves Ashley with the 4.31 p.m. Manchester–Chester train on 3 May 1947. These engines, designed by Pollitt, had spent the best part of fifty years on the CLC system providing sterling service, but none survived to see the year out. (*J.D. Darby*)

Another diverted express is seen passing Ashley station during electrification works on the Manchester–Crewe line. 'Royal Scot' 4–6–0, no. 46154 *The Hussar*, is at the head of a Manchester–Bristol express on 28 July 1957. (*David Chatfield*)

A lengthy freight in the hands of two MS&LR types, J10 0–6–0, no. 5166 (BR 65166), and N5 0–6–2 tank, no. 69281, approaches Ashley in the direction of Northwich on 26 June 1948. (*J.D. Darby*)

The climb out of Altrincham towards Hale presents a challenge to heavier trains such as those carrying the limestone loads. In this picture from 1959, Stanier class 5 4–6–0, no. 45404, is working hard to lift its Easter Sunday excursion away from the town and on to Llandudno.
(David Chatfield)

In this period piece, the steam train is seen in the context of daily life in the 1950s. The location is Hale station and the local road traffic has come to a halt as ex-GCR D11, no. 62662 *Prince of Wales*, departs with a Manchester Central–Chester Northgate train in about 1957.
(Doug Rendell)

Approaching Altrincham from the north, a Fowler 2–6–4 tank, no. 42417, enters the station with a Manchester Central–Chester Northgate service on 9 June 1957. This engine was based at Chester at the time. Altrincham was the southern terminus of the MSJ&AR electric line to Manchester and most of the electric trains used the lines to the left to gain access to the station.
(David Chatfield)

At Deansgate Junction, a line branches away eastwards to Skelton Junction where it met the CLC and LNWR lines from Warrington. On the MSJ&AR line at Deansgate Junction, a Midland Railway 3F 0–6–0, no. 43457, is seen working wrong line with a works train in April 1957. *(T. Noble/David Chatfield Collection)*

Another Chester–Manchester service passes Timperley Junction in the hands of Stanier 2–6–4 tank, no. 42467, on 8 September 1957. The line joining from the right is the LNWR route from Warrington Bank Quay Low Level, while the line on the viaduct in the background is the CLC route from Warrington Central to Stockport and Godley Junction. *(T. Noble/David Chatfield Collection)*

Brooklands station in Sale is the location as a Robinson 'Director' D10 4–4–0, no. 62656 *Sir Clement Royds*, passes through with the 6.40 p.m. Manchester Central–Chester Northgate service on 5 June 1954. Like other GCR 4–4–0s such as the D6s and D9s before them and the very similar D11s that arrived at about the same time, these locomotives spent most of their final years on the CLC system. (*T. Noble/David Chatfield Collection*)

Cheshire plays host to Lancashire & Yorkshire motive power as L&YR 2–4–2 tank, no. 50705, having called at Sale station, departs with the 7.12 p.m. to Warrington Bank Quay (Low Level) on 14 August 1956. The train will leave the MSJ&AR route at Timperley Junction and head west through Broadheath and Thelwall. The engine was based at Warrington. (*David Chatfield*)

Leaving Sale behind, a Hughes 'Crab' 2–6–0, no. 42818, is approaching Dane Road station at the north end of Sale near to the Cheshire boundary on 19 May 1956. This engine was one of five fitted with rotary valve gear in 1931 but this was later replaced with Reidinger valve gear. *(David Chatfield)*

4

Cross-country Routes in North Cheshire

The first of the cross-country routes across north Cheshire was, as might be expected, an LNWR line. In 1851, an independent company, the Warrington & Altrincham Junction Railway, obtained authority to build a line from Arpley, where it would connect with the St Helens Railway, to Timperley, on the MSJ&AR. In 1853 it obtained a further act to authorise an extension to Stockport and the company became the Warrington & Stockport Railway to reflect its greater ambition. The line opened initially in 1853 and was connected to the St Helens Railway at Arpley and the MSJ&AR near Broadheath in 1854. The further connection to the WCML at Walton Junction was completed in 1855. Lack of capital prevented the company from extending eastwards to Stockport and, furthermore, the LNWR objected to the running powers into Manchester via Timperley. The dispute was prolonged, resulting in a settlement in 1860 whereby the LNWR agreed to lease the Warrington & Stockport.

Although the Warrington & Stockport Railway had failed to achieve its ultimate aim, the gap from Altrincham to Stockport was completed in 1866. Stockport had already gained an easterly connection to the MS&LR's line to Marple, via the Stockport & Woodley Junction line that had opened in 1863. Although only a short line of 2¾ miles, it was significant in that it gave added impetus to an east–west route through Stockport, especially as the line between Altrincham and Northwich was about to open and a connection between Northwich and Helsby had been authorised. The possibility of access to the port of Birkenhead as well as the salt and chemical industries near Northwich was within sight. With active support from the MS&LR, an act was obtained for a new company, the Stockport, Timperley & Altrincham Junction Railway, to build a line which linked the Stockport–Woodley Junction line at Portwood, just east of Stockport, with the MSJ&AR at Deansgate Junction, north of Altrincham. It opened on 1 December 1865. An additional connection from Skelton Junction to Broadheath (LNWR territory) was opened on 1 February 1866. The MS&LR, together with the GNR, had already reached agreement in 1863 by virtue of the Great Northern (Cheshire Lines) Act to manage the four lines that made up the route from Woodley Junction to Helsby via Stockport, Altrincham and Northwich.

The Midland Railway, who were interested in acquiring a share of the Liverpool traffic, too, became a third partner in the committee that achieved legal independence as the Cheshire Lines Committee in 1867. The cross-country route was completed when the CLC extended their line westwards from Skelton Junction via Glazebrook to Cressington Junction (and hence to Brunswick, Liverpool) in 1873, shortly before the opening of its direct route from Manchester Oxford Road (but Manchester Central station from 1880) to Liverpool.

The significance of the CLC cross-country route can be gauged by the number of junctions along its length of over 18 miles. From Godley Junction, the line passed through Apethorne Junction, Woodley Junction, Bredbury Junction, Brinnington Junction, Heaton Mersey East Junction, Cheadle Junction, Northenden Junction, Skelton Junction and Glazebrook East Junction, amounting to, on average, one junction every 2 miles. With connections to what would become the GCR, the Midland Railway and the LNWR, it is little wonder that this line saw such a variety of locomotive types until the last decade of steam.

Of the two cross-country routes across north Cheshire, it was the Warrington–Timperley Junction line that was first on the scene. An LMS 'Crab' 2-6-0, no.42705, heads eastwards with a fitted freight on 19 September 1961 at about 4.15 p.m. In the distance is Latchford viaduct spanning the Manchester Ship Canal. *(Michael Mensing)*

Opposite, top: On 15 May 1948, a Stanier class 3 2–6–2 tank engine, no. 106, in LMS livery, stops at Thelwall station with the 4.55 p.m. Saturdays Manchester–Warrington service. *(J.D. Darby)*

Opposite, bottom: In the final year of service, a Manchester–Warrington motor train leaves Dunham Massey with BR Standard class 2 2–6–2 tank, no. 84001, pushing from the rear on 28 July 1962. Note the tall signal designed to give improved visibility to the engine crew and evidence that this picture was taken from a bridge, which otherwise would have hampered visibility. *(David Chatfield)*

With little more than ten months to go before the end of the steam era on BR, a Stanier class 8F 2–8–0, no. 48745, trundles a Guide Bridge–Garston mineral train past Broadheath on 7 October 1967. *(John Hilton)*

Another Warrington–Manchester service is seen, this time dropping down the curve from Broadheath Junction to Timperley Junction on the MSJ&AR on 28 July 1962. The engine in charge is an LMS class 2 2–6–2 tank, no. 41213. The line to the left of the signal-box continues from Warrington towards Stockport. *(David Chatfield)*

The 6.20 a.m. Warrington–Manchester with Stanier class 3 2–6–2 tank, no. 40107, at the head, has reached the bottom of the spur from Broadheath Junction and now meets the MSJ&AR at Timperley Junction in April 1952. The viaduct in the background is the CLC route between Warrington Central and Stockport. *(J.D. Darby)*

East of Broadheath Junction the line was built in stages from Godley to Portwood in Stockport and then on to Deansgate Junction where it met the MSJ&AR. Afterwards, a line was built to join on to the LNWR route at Broadheath Junction. Where the lines from Broadheath and Deansgate Junction met was at Skelton Junction and this is where we see Stanier 8F 2–8–0, no. 48503, with an Ellesmere Port–Tuxford oil train on 24 June 1967. The train is negotiating the junction with the other cross-country line, the later CLC route from Liverpool and Warrington Central. *(John Hilton)*

Superpower is in evidence at Skelton Junction as two BR class 9 2–10–0s, nos 92117 and 92106, approach from Broadheath with a Stanlow–Leeds oil train on 15 April 1967. From Skelton Junction the two cross-country lines head eastwards as one line. *(John Hilton)*

In the final year of steam on BR, a Stanier 8F 2–8–0, no. 48252 of Heaton Mersey shed, passes Skelton Junction and its tall signal-box with a Garston–Spink Hill mineral train on 6 April 1968. *(John Hilton)*

The signal-box seen in the last picture can be seen at Skelton Junction in the background. The passenger train is the diverted 3.15 p.m. Manchester London Road–Bristol express hauled by Stanier class 5 4–6–0, no. 45390, which is making its way round the curve to Deansgate Junction on 25 March 1956. The Warrington lines lie to the right while, in between, is the extensive goods yard and turntable. (*T. Noble/David Chatfield Collection*)

Approaching Skelton Junction from the east is an ex-Franco Crosti-boilered BR class 9F 2–10–0, no. 92021, with oil wagons from Leeds to Stanlow on 20 May 1967. (*John Hilton*)

On CLC territory, the first stop east of Skelton Junction was at Baguley where Stanier class 4 2–6–4 tank, no. 42445, arrives with the noon Liverpool Central–Stockport Tiviot Dale passenger on 27 April 1963. Note the line crossing behind the left-hand platform into the small goods bay to the rear of the station. *(David Chatfield)*

In this overview of Baguley station, the goods yard at the rear of the station can be seen with a MS&LR J10 0–6–0, no. 65194, signalled to rejoin the main line where the rest of its train is waiting on 15 April 1950. Note the cattle dock in the left foreground. *(David Chatfield)*

In this final view of Baguley station, the goods bay with cattle dock in the background can be seen to the right as Midland Railway 2P 4–4–0, no. 40464, prepares to depart with a train from Stockport on 7 October 1950. (*J.D. Darby*)

An early BR scene sees GCR D10 4–4–0, no. 2653 (BR 62653) *Sir Edward Fraser*, between Northenden and Baguley, with the 3.23 p.m. from Stockport on 26 June 1948. (*J.D. Darby*)

The diverted 2.30 p.m. Manchester London Road–Birmingham express hauled by a 'Royal Scot', no. 46111 *Royal Fusilier*, in splendid condition, passes Northenden station on 18 March 1956. The station board refers to Wythenshawe, a reminder that this section of line actually lies outside the county boundary. It is included for the sake of continuity. *(John Hilton)*

Northenden Junction is where the lines split up again with the LNWR route veering to the right towards Stockport Edgeley and Buxton, while the CLC route continues towards Stockport Tiviot Dale and Godley Junction. Approaching from Tiviot Dale is a GCR D9, no. 2321, with a Warrington service composed of what appears to be old CLC non-corridor stock on 27 April 1948. *(J.D. Darby)*

Briefly following the LNWR lines to the right in the previous picture, the Styal line is reached. Here, a Stanier 8F 2–8–0, no. 8745, heads a coal train towards Northenden Junction on 7 August 1948. The Styal line crosses above in the background while the chimneys of Stockport can be seen in the distance. Today, the M56 and M60 motorways meet in this vicinity. *(J.D. Darby)*

Returning to the CLC line, we see the 3.23 p.m. Stockport Tiviot Dale–Warrington train, hauled by Stanier class 3 2–6–2 tank, no. 40203, after arrival at Cheadle station on 20 September 1951. *(Ron Gee)*

An LMS 4–4–0 Compound, no. 41112, passes Heaton Mersey on the approach to Stockport and the next stop at Tiviot Dale on 24 April 1954. Heaton Mersey shed can be seen in the distance behind the rear coach. *(T. Noble/David Chatfield Collection)*

The M60 motorway sweeps through this part of Stockport today but the site was once occupied by Stockport Tiviot Dale. A Stanier class 4 2–6–4 tank, no. 42598, waits at the Up platform with a Liverpool Central train on 12 June 1954. There was a regular service to Warrington and Liverpool Central and no. 42598 was often employed on this train until the service was withdrawn in 1964. It was based at Liverpool's Brunswick depot until that shed's closure in 1961 whereupon it moved to Speke depot. *(T. Noble/David Chatfield Collection)*

At the east end of Tiviot Dale, a Fairburn 2–6–4 tank, no. 42134, of Heaton Mersey depot, ambles through the station's centre roads, probably returning to its depot on 23 March 1963. The Fairburn locomotives were very similar to the Stanier 2–6–4 tanks, the most obvious difference being the break in the running plate in front of the cylinders on the Fairburn engines. *(Peter Fitton)*

Against a back-cloth of mills, an Ivatt class 4 2–6–0, no. 43048, of Heaton Mersey depot, canters down grade through Tiviot Dale on 23 March 1963 with a westbound freight, possibly destined for the yards at Heaton Mersey. *(Peter Fitton)*

Since passing Bredbury Junction, WD 2–8–0, no. 90342, has climbed to Woodley Junction and enjoyed a brief respite in the short distance down to Apethorne Junction where it is held at signals. Another 2 miles at 1 in 100 lies in front of the train as it waits for the road to Godley Junction on 31 August 1965. The line to the left leads to Hyde Junction on the Manchester–Sheffield electrified route. *(Peter Fitton)*

Opposite, top: Another Heaton Mersey-based Ivatt class 4 2–6–0, no. 43031, from the Woodley direction, passes the compact signal-box at Bredbury Junction on its way towards Stockport and Heaton Mersey on 9 October 1965. The lines joining from the right are from Romiley and were used by the Midland Railway's London trains until its direct route through Cheadle Heath was opened. The viaduct in the background carries the line from Piccadilly to Sheffield, the first Midland route into Manchester. This will join the lines to the right at Romiley. *(Peter Fitton)*

Opposite, bottom: Another view of Bredbury Junction, taken from the opposite direction, sees BR Standard class 9 ex-Franco Crosti-boilered, no. 92027, begin the stiff climb at 1 in 61 to Woodley Junction with a Runcorn–Worksop coal empties on 30 September 1965. At Godley Junction, no. 92027 will give way to electric power. *(Peter Fitton)*

A BR class 4 2–6–0, no. 76087, of Heaton Mersey shed, arrives at Godley Junction with the 2.40 p.m.
Manchester Central–Leicester on 20 May 1962. The former Great Central main line from Manchester to
Sheffield can be seen on the right. *(John Hilton)*

5

North-East Cheshire

When Travis Street opened in 1840 it was the third Manchester terminus after Liverpool Road and Oldham Road. It was the temporary terminus of the Manchester & Birmingham's route to Stockport – the first stage of a grand plan to build a shorter route to London. That company agreed to share Travis Street station with the Sheffield, Ashton-under-Lyne & Manchester Railway (SA&MR), whose new route as far as Godley opened on 17 November 1841. Like the M&BR, it had more ambitious plans – in this case to reach Sheffield.

Both these railways made progress through Cheshire in the following year by which time Travis Street had been replaced by London Road station. From Stockport the line had now reached Crewe and from Godley the eastern route had been extended to Broadbottom, before arriving at Woodhead in 1844. A branch was built from the SA&MR's station at Guide Bridge (originally Ashton) to Stalybridge in 1845 where it would eventually form a junction with the LNWR, which had opened its line from Stalybridge to Huddersfield in 1849. By this time the SA&MR had become the MS&LR (from 1847), and there followed a period of consolidation during which Edward Watkin joined the company as general manager in 1854. He had made his name as an LNWR employee, and in the face of that company's aggressive stance towards potential competitors in their territory, he began to develop relations with the GNR. This led to an agreement in 1857 that allowed trains from London King's Cross to reach Manchester London Road via Retford, where the MS&LR's cross-country route met the GNR's main line to Doncaster. This agreement infuriated the LNWR but it only served to strengthen the resolve of the two smaller companies. The MS&LR and GNR set about lending their support to other railway schemes that would, in time, give them a route to Liverpool, as referred to in the last chapter. In the meantime the LNWR had begun to extend eastwards from Stockport with a line that initially ran to Whaley Bridge in 1857. This had caused concern to the Midland Railway who had been seeking a route in the other direction towards Manchester. The MS&LR was approached with a view to facilitating this access and this led to the opening of a new route via New Mills in 1865 to join the with the MS&LR's extension from Hyde via Woodley to Marple. The new line was a joint project between the MS&LR and the Midland Railway who, in 1866, had become the third member of the CLC. By this move it, too, gained a route to Merseyside. The MS&LR had also co-operated with the NSR in 1871 in running the Marple–Macclesfield line that had been opened two years earlier.

In 1875, the Midland Railway found a more direct route into Manchester London Road when, in conjunction with the MS&LR, it opened a line from Romiley, on the Hyde–Marple line, to Ashburys, on the Sheffield line near London Road. There were connections to Stockport, which proved useful when London Road became congested and the Midland Railway was forced to look for an alternative route into Manchester via Heaton Mersey and Chorlton to Manchester Central. Much of this new route lay mainly outside Cheshire's boundaries but when the Midland sought even better access into the city it chose a route that followed a similar path to that of the LNWR line into Derbyshire. It left its existing line at New Mills South Junction and passed through Disley tunnel, Hazel Grove and Cheadle Heath to Heaton Mersey Junction. The line opened in 1902 thus completing the railway network in this part of Cheshire.

The first line to open in this part of Cheshire was the line from Manchester to Godley. It entered Cheshire to the east of Guide Bridge (the boundary line following the River Tame) and then left again to the east of Mottram (the boundary following the River Etherow). This line was eventually extended to Sheffield and, decades later, would reach London Marylebone. In terms of motive power, some would argue that the golden era was when LNER A3 Pacifics handled some of the London trains. At Hyde Junction, for instance, we see Gresley A3, no. 60049 *Galtee More*, with the 2.40 p.m. Manchester–London express on 18 April 1951. *(J.D. Darby)*

Opposite, top: On the same day, a Thompson B1, no. 61315, climbs past Hyde Junction with the Liverpool Central–Harwich boat train. The gradient at this point is 1 in 97 but the climb out of Manchester London Road is unrelenting for most of the 22 miles to Dunford Bridge, east of the Woodhead Tunnel, making it one of the most arduous of starts from any main line station. *(J.D. Darby)*

Opposite, bottom: On a wet day, the 3.50 p.m. Manchester–London storms past Godley with Thompson B1, no. 61187, in charge on 31 March 1951. The climb will ease a little on the approach to Mottram, the next station along the line, but it will be a challenge given the prevailing conditions. The lines from Stockport are out of sight to the left of the near platform. *(J.D. Darby)*

In this view towards the Cheshire/Derbyshire border, a London–Manchester express passes through Mottram cutting with another Gresley A3 4–6–2, no. 60054 *Prince of Wales*, in charge in May 1953. Several of these locomotives were transferred to the Great Central line in 1938 and, for a time, there was an allocation at Gorton including *Flying Scotsman*. The A3s worked along this line until electrification to Sheffield Victoria was completed in 1954. In this picture the gantries have been erected already. (*David Chatfield*)

A Thompson B1 4–6–0, no. 61182, of Gorton shed, passes through Mottram and Broadbottom station with an Up freight on 3 June 1950. (*J.D. Darby*)

On the same day, sister engine, no. 61184, also from Gorton, approaches Mottram and Broadbottom station from the opposite direction with the 3.20 p.m. Sheffield Victoria–Manchester London Road. (J.D. Darby)

Another B1, no. 61159, at the head of the 9.55 a.m. Manchester–Cleethorpes express, passes Broadbottom village, close to the border with Derbyshire on 2 May 1953. It appears to be carrying an unidentified nameboard and, as this locomotive would have been a regular visitor to Sheffield Victoria, it is possible that the board is either that of the 'Master Cutler' or 'The South Yorkshireman'. (J.D. Darby)

Beyond Mottram the line passes into Derbyshire but, surprisingly, returns to Cheshire at Woodhead; indeed, a significant portion of the Woodhead Tunnel was in Cheshire. The rugged nature of this part of the county is seen from the Derbyshire side of the border as another B1, no. 61313, climbs past Torside with the Manchester London Road–Sheffield Victoria express on 5 June 1954, one week before electric workings commenced. *(David Chatfield)*

On the Derbyshire/Cheshire border, a Gresley V2 2–6–2, no. 60863, eases out of the tunnel and past the station at Woodhead with a Manchester express on 5 June 1954. *(David Chatfield)*

The mills of Stalybridge give an impression of Lancashire rather than Cheshire and as if to confirm this illusion, an Aspinall 0–6–0, no. 52455, of Lancashire & Yorkshire Railway origin, based at Newton Heath, is seen with a freight train to the west of the station on 30 May 1956. (*John Hilton*)

At Stalybridge station, a Gorton-based C13 4–4–2 tank, no. 67417, is in charge of a push-pull set for Oldham Clegg Street via Guide Bridge on 27 December 1958. No. 67417 was the last survivor of its class when withdrawn in 1959. (*David Chatfield*)

From Hyde Junction, less than 2 miles to the east of Guide Bridge, the MS&LR opened a branch to Hyde in 1858 and this was extended to Marple in 1862. It was later operated jointly with the Midland Railway to provide the latter company with access to Manchester. A Fairburn 2–6–4 tank, no. 42248, of Gorton shed, has arrived at Hyde North station with the diverted Sundays-only 2.40 p.m. Manchester Piccadilly–Leicester on 20 May 1962. Hyde Junction is in the background and the electrified wires of the Sheffield route can be seen in front of the buildings to the right of the engine. *(John Hilton)*

Continuing from Hyde, Apethorne Junction is reached. It was encountered in the previous chapter on the cross-country journey to Godley, the line to which branches away to the right. With the mills of Hyde in the background, a Stanier 2–6–0, no. 42977, crosses the junction with a westbound freight on 31 August 1965. *(Peter Fitton)*

From Apethorne Junction we continue through Woodley Junction (where the cross-country CLC route branches away to the west) and curve south to Romiley, where the direct route from London Road and the lines from Tiviot Dale were joined. In this bird's eye view of the approach to Romiley, we see a Thompson B1, no. 1029 *Chamois*, still in LNER livery, with the 12.22 p.m. London Road–New Mills train on 19 February 1949. On the left are the lines climbing from Stockport Tiviot Dale and Bredbury Junction while, just visible at a higher level on the right, is the line from Hyde Junction and Woodley. *(J.D. Darby)*

This picture was taken from the same location but at a lower level and shows a MS&LR J10 0–6–0, no. 65157, climbing towards Romiley from Bredbury Junction with a coal train on 19 February 1949. The direct line from London Road can be seen to the right. No. 65157 was a Heaton Mersey engine at the time and became one of the last two of its class when withdrawn towards the end of 1961 from Springs Branch, Wigan. *(J.D. Darby)*

Another view of the meeting of the three routes into Romiley shows a Stanier class 5 4–6–0, no. 44735, of Trafford Park shed, climbing from Bredbury Junction in charge of the 1.45 p.m. Manchester Central–Sheffield on 30 September 1965. *(Peter Fitton)*

An LNER B1 4–6–0, no. 61160, arrives at Romiley station with the 12.22 p.m. Manchester London Road–New Mills train on 15 March 1952. *(J.D. Darby)*

Another view of Romiley station shows the station staff posing beside Stanier 'Silver Jubilee', no. 45602 *British Honduras*, on the 10.50 a.m. Manchester Central–Sheffield train on 16 March 1952. The locomotive bears the shed plate for Bristol Barrow Road. *(Ron Gee)*

A Robinson J11 0–6–0, no. 64346, rumbles past Romiley station with the 9.45 a.m. Godley–Hayfield goods train on 16 March 1952. The line from Bredbury Junction can be seen joining from the left. This Great Central Railway locomotive was allocated to Gorton at the time. *(Ron Gee)*

At Marple Wharf Junction the line splits, with the GCR & North Staffordshire Railway Joint Line to Macclesfield veering south, away from the GCR & Midland Joint Line to New Mills. In this picture at Marple Wharf Viaduct, a Hughes 'Crab' 2–6–0, no. 42890, is seen pulling away from the junction, just beyond the viaduct, with an excursion train for Belle Vue on 26 May 1958. To the right runs the Peak Forest Canal with textile sheds, complete with their 'northlight' roofs, situated alongside. *(A.C. Gilbert)*

Further along the route to New Mills, a Stanier 'Jubilee', no. 45600 *Bermuda*, based at Newton Heath shed, passes Marple station with an eastbound freight near to the border with Derbyshire on 9 October 1965. *(Peter Fitton)*

Returning to Marple Wharf Junction and proceeding now to Macclesfield, the first station along this line was Marple Rose Hill. Arriving at this station on 22 March 1952 is a GCR J11 0–6–0, no. 64440, with the 3.05 p.m. Manchester London Road–Macclesfield Central. *(Ron Gee)*

Having crossed over the LNWR line to Buxton, the journey south takes in Higher Poynton station where another J11 0–6–0, no. 64316, calls with the 3.05 p.m. train from Manchester on 6 June 1953. *(J.D. Darby)*

Another Robinson design for the Great Central Railway was the A5 4–6–2 tank and here we see no. 69817 at Bollington station with a service from Manchester, via Reddish and Bredbury, bound for Macclesfield Central on 4 May 1957. (*John Hilton*)

In this final view of the Macclesfield route from Manchester London Road via Romiley, we see a Fowler 2–6–4 tank, no. 42374, leaving Bollington with the 1.05 p.m. from Manchester on 27 March 1959. The locomotive was allocated to Gorton depot at a time when ex-LMS types were beginning to take over the duties of former LNER classes (especially those of GCR origin). Textile mills, such as the one in the background at Bollington, were a common sight in the towns on the eastern side of Cheshire. (*Michael Mensing*)

The only LNWR route from Cheshire into Derbyshire was the Buxton line that caused much agitation among its competitors and was a factor in the Midland Railway's co-operation with the MS&LR in finding a route to Manchester via Marple. The line left the Manchester–Crewe main line at Edgeley, south of Stockport station. Leaving the main line on 12 July 1955 is a Fowler 2–6–4 tank, no. 42365, with the 4.00 p.m. Manchester London Road–Buxton service. *(John Hilton)*

In the south-eastern suburbs of Stockport, a Stanier 8F 2–8–0, no. 48613, with flat-sided green tender, passes Bramhall Moor Lane with a freight on 15 July 1958. *(David Chatfield)*

It is uphill most of the way as a Hughes 'Crab' 2–6–0, no. 42943, of Buxton shed, heads a freight through Hazel Grove in the direction of its home town in March 1957. *(David Chatfield)*

Soon after leaving Hazel Grove, the railway leaves the urban landscape behind and, by the time it reaches Middlewood Low Level station, the surroundings are open countryside. The 12.10 p.m. Manchester London Road–Buxton service has arrived at the snow-laden platform at Middlewood behind a Longsight-based Fowler 2–6–4 tank, no. 42399, 16 February 1957. These engines were associated with this service for many years. Beyond the train is the bridge carrying the jointly owned Macclesfield line, referred to earlier. *(John Hilton)*

The last major railway development in this part of Cheshire was the Midland Railway's main line from New Mills South to Heaton Mersey, where access was gained to Manchester Central station. At the north end of Cheadle Heath, a spur branched away from the main line to join the CLC route between Stockport and Skelton Junction. In this picture a Fairburn 2–6–4 tank, no. 42159, approaches the station with a stopping train from Manchester Central on 27 July 1963. The spur to the CLC route can be seen on the left while in the distance, beyond the last three coaches, can be seen the level course of another spur from the main line joining the CLC route to Stockport Tiviot Dale at Heaton Mersey. *(D. Forsyth/ P. Chancellor Collection)*

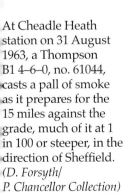

At Cheadle Heath station on 31 August 1963, a Thompson B1 4–6–0, no. 61044, casts a pall of smoke as it prepares for the 15 miles against the grade, much of it at 1 in 100 or steeper, in the direction of Sheffield. *(D. Forsyth/ P. Chancellor Collection)*

On the Midland Main Line at Hazel Grove there is ample power to haul a four-coach train on 1 March 1951. The Stanier class 5 4–6–0, no. 44815, based at Derby, is seen piloting an LMS Compound. (J.D. Darby)

Opposite, top: Cheadle Heath in earlier times as Fowler 4F 0–6–0, no. 4286 (later 44286), in LMS livery, eases out of the station with a mixed freight bound for Derbyshire on 10 May 1948. In the large goods yard (now a retail park) to the left, a Deeley 3F 0–6–0 is shunting wagons. *(J.D. Darby)*

Opposite, bottom: A 'Silver Jubilee' 4–6–0, no. 45705 *Seahorse*, stands at the south end of Cheadle Heath station in readiness to work a special train to Birmingham on 18 September 1965. The locomotive had spent much of its life at Farnley Junction (near Leeds) and at Blackpool before moving to the Manchester area. It was based at Trafford Park shed when photographed and had been regularly used on the Buxton–Manchester Central commuter trains. The stripe on the cabside was worn by many steam locomotives at this time and acted as a prohibition against working along the electrified wires south of Crewe because of insufficient clearances. *(Peter Fitton)*

This last look at the Midland Main Line through Cheshire sees another Stanier class 5 4–6–0, no. 45101, emerging from Disley Tunnel with an Up express, 2 August 1958. *(G.M. Shoults/J.D. Darby Collection)*

6

Manchester's routes to London Euston and the North Staffordshire

Given the circuitous route from Manchester's first station at Liverpool Road to London, it was only a matter of time before a more convenient route would be proposed. In fact, two companies, the Manchester & Cheshire Junction and the Manchester South Union, planned to build lines towards the Midlands and London. Due to opposition from the GJR, a more modest project was agreed involving the merging of the fledgling companies as the Manchester & Birmingham Railway. Its revised proposal to join the main line at Crewe received the blessing of the established company.

While this line opened to Crewe in 1842, a branch was built to Macclesfield, opening in 1845, just at the time when a series of railway developments in the Potteries was about to be authorised by Parliament. Crucially, these included a line from Macclesfield to Colwich, similar to the original scheme of the Manchester South Union Railway that was intended to meet the main line to London in the Midlands. From authorisation in 1846 to completion took a mere three years, by which time the Trent Valley line from Rugby to Stafford had been opened. Thus, a new, more direct route became available from Manchester to London. It should be added that it was not until 1859 that the NSR and the LNWR reached agreement on traffic arrangements, resulting in the routing of some LNWR trains through Macclesfield to Euston. The same agreement saw NSR locomotives working into Manchester London Road.

In 1849, when the through route from Macclesfield to Colwich opened, a further line opened from North Rode, north of Congleton, through the Churnet Valley to Uttoxeter. The NSR's route from Stoke to Crewe had opened in the previous year while further NSR branches reached into Cheshire in the course of time. The branch from Lawton Junction (on the Stoke–Crewe line) to Sandbach opened in stages between 1852 and 1866, the branch from Stoke to Congleton via Biddulph opened in 1859 to goods traffic, and the jointly operated line (between the MS&LR and NSR) from Marple to Macclesfield opened in 1869.

Apart from the two London routes via Stockport, mention has already been made of the service from Manchester London Road to King's Cross via the MS&LR's Sheffield line and Retford. This operated later from Manchester Central. The service ceased during the First World War but, by that time, two new routes were in operation. The GCR began its service following completion of its route to London Marylebone in 1899. It was the building of this line that prompted the MS&LR to change its name to the GCR. Finally, the Midland Railway opened its direct route from Manchester Central to London St Pancras in 1902.

Today, the two oldest routes survive via Crewe and via Stoke, with regular London trains.

The approach to Stockport Edgeley station from Manchester is via the impressive viaduct that crosses the Mersey valley. In the period before electrification of the route, a BR 'Britannia' 4–6–2, no. 70031 *Byron*, arrives at Stockport with the 8.10 a.m. Manchester London Road–London Euston express on 1 August 1958. The CLC route to Stockport Tiviot Dale, just outside the Cheshire boundary, runs unseen below the viaduct. *(John Hilton)*

A little later on the same day, an unrebuilt and unnamed 'Patriot' 4–6–0, no. 45544, departs from Stockport and is about to cross the viaduct with the 7.50 a.m. Buxton–Manchester London Road commuter train. Mills and their chimneys abound in this industrial scene. *(John Hilton)*

Children are drawn to a Stanier class 5 4–6–0, no. 44860, as it waits for departure from the north end of Stockport Edgeley station on Saturday 9 April 1960 at 5.04 p.m. The train engine has just parted company with its pilot engine, Stanier class 5 4–6–0, no. 44909, which seems curious bearing in mind that the train was just 5 miles from Manchester. Equally interesting is that both locomotives were based at Rugby. Is it possible that the original train engine failed in the vicinity of Rugby and that no. 44860 will take the route east of Manchester to Victoria station, not uncommon during the months leading up to electrification of the Manchester–Crewe line? (*Michael Mensing*)

One of Stockport's allocation of Bowen-Cooke 0–8–0s designed for the LNWR, no. 49010, awaits the road with a short freight on 6 August 1958 while a Stanier class 5 4–6–0 occupies the other centre road with coaches and wagons. (*David Chatfield*)

An early Stanier design was his class 2P 0–4–4 'Push-Pull' tank of which only ten were built from 1932. Longsight shed had a small allocation, including no. 41907, during the 1950s. It is seen here leaving one of Stockport's bay platforms at the southern end of the station with the 2.11 p.m. Stockport–Alderley Edge train on 14 October 1956. *(J.D. Darby)*

At Edgeley Junction, the Buxton line diverged to the south-east while another LNWR line veered to the west to meet the CLC route at Northenden Junction. Seen looking towards Stockport from the south, one of Longsight's rebuilt 'Patriot' 4–6–0s, no. 45540 *Sir Robert Turnbull*, with the 9.45 a.m. London-bound 'Mancunian', passes Edgeley no.1 box on 20 July 1956. This train usually avoided Stockport by taking the Styal line to Wilmslow but was, presumably, diverted because of the early stages of electrification on that line. The Buxton lines can be seen diverging to the right in the foreground. *(J.D. Darby)*

Another view at the same location sees an original Franco Crosti-boilered class 9F 2–10–0, no. 92025, near Edgeley Junction with the 6.20 a.m. Hull–Crewe goods on 14 July 1955. The exhaust on this engine was ejected from the funnel on the side instead of at the front end but all ten of these engines were later converted to conventional operation. The engine here is barely two months old and, as it has not been supplied with a shed code, it is assumed that at this stage it is still undergoing proving trials before allocation to Wellingborough depot. (*John Hilton*)

A Pacific in ex-works condition suggests a running-in turn for 'Princess Royal' 4–6–2, no. 46204 *Princess Louise*, with the 7.53 p.m. Crewe–Manchester London Road approaching Edgeley no. 1 box on 12 July 1955. (*John Hilton*)

Also approaching Edgeley Junction is a Hughes 'Crab' 2–6–0, no. 42703, with the 6.00 a.m. Stafford–Manchester London Road on 13 May 1958. The Buxton lines trail away to the left and Edgeley yard can be seen in the background to the right of the locomotive. *(J.D. Darby)*

South of Edgeley Junction, a 'Princess Coronation' Pacific, no. 46223 *Princess Alice*, of Polmadie shed in Glasgow, gathers speed with the 11.10 a.m. Manchester London Road–Crewe stopping train on 15 October 1956. Judging by its condition, this locomotive, too, appears to be engaged in a running-in turn following overhaul at Crewe Works. *(J.D. Darby)*

An interesting visitor to Stockport is BR Standard class 9F 2–10–0, no. 92079, the Lickey banker complete with spotlight, waiting for the passage of a Down express while on a Crewe–Guide Bridge freight at Edgeley Junction on 3 April 1958. It is assumed that this run is in connection with a visit to Crewe Works. *(John Hilton)*

A Fowler 7F 0–8–0, no. 49509, leaves Edgeley goods yard with the 10.15 a.m. freight for Diggle on the LNWR Manchester–Huddersfield route on 31 May 1955. *(J.D. Darby)*

A Fowler 2–6–4 tank, no. 42343, is seen in pristine condition at Stockport Edgeley shed on 23 March 1963. A WD 2–8–0, no. 90110, can be seen behind the tank engine. *(Peter Fitton)*

The next station south of Stockport is Cheadle Hulme where the London line via Stoke veers away. Approaching on the main line to Crewe is an unidentified Fowler 2–6–4 tank with an express on 28 August 1954. *(T. Noble/David Chatfield Collection)*

Wilmslow is where the lines from Stockport and Styal meet. Two of Wilmslow's four platforms can be seen in this view, shortly before the inauguration of electric services between Manchester and Crewe. A Stanier class 5 4–6–0, no. 45311, arrives with the 12.10 p.m. from Manchester London Road on 18 April 1960. (*T. Noble/David Chatfield Collection*)

Much of the line via Styal lies outside the Cheshire boundary but in this view we see a Manchester Longsight 'Royal Scot' 4–6–0, no. 46160 *Queen Victoria's Rifleman*, at the head of the 9.45 a.m. Up 'Mancunian', speeding through Heald Green station on 11 March 1954. (*Ron Gee*)

A little further south a Stanier class 3 2–6–2 tank engine, no. 40093, approaches Styal with the 3.43 p.m. Manchester London Road–Alderley Edge on 22 May 1957. (*J.D. Darby*)

Returning to the main line, we are now south of Alderley Edge on Good Friday 27 March 1959 when a Sunday service was effectively in operation. One of Longsight's 'Silver Jubilees', no. 45638 *Zanzibar*, is in charge of the 10.30 a.m. from Manchester London Road with through-coaches for Cardiff and Kingswear. At Crewe the train will take the line to Shrewsbury where the train will divide. (*Michael Mensing*)

On the main line south of Wilmslow, 'The Mancunian' is seen near Chelford behind BR 'Britannia' 4–6–2, no. 70032 *Tennyson*, on 5 September 1953. *(T. Noble/David Chatfield Collection)*

A Stanier 'Jubilee' 4–6–0, no. 45723 *Fearless*, at the head of an excursion train, crosses Peover Viaduct between Chelford and Goostrey on 4 June 1953. *(T. Noble/David Chatfield Collection)*

A Stanier 'Princess Royal' Pacific, no. 46210 *Lady Patricia*, is captured on film near Goostrey on 3 August 1953 with a local turn, in between more prestigious duties from its base at Crewe. *(T. Noble/David Chatfield Collection)*

Between Holmes Chapel and Sandbach, a 'Royal Scot' 4–6–0, no. 46131 *The Royal Warwickshire Regiment*, heads south along the Cheshire plain with the Sundays 4.00 p.m. Manchester London Road–London Euston on 2 September 1951. *(John Hilton)*

Returning to Cheadle Hulme to follow the London route via Macclesfield, we see another 'Royal Scot' 4–6–0, no. 46120 *Royal Inniskilling Fusilier,* on the 'Pines Express' on 5 September 1954. *(T. Noble/David Chatfield Collection)*

'Royal Scot' 4–6–0, no. 46161 *King's Own,* in charge of the 2.25 p.m. Manchester London Road–Birmingham New Street, emerges from the tunnel at the north end of Prestbury station and makes good progress along the rising gradient on Good Friday, 27 March 1959. In fact, it is almost continuously uphill for 12 miles from Cheadle Hulme to beyond Macclesfield at gradients mainly varying between 1 in 150 and 1 in 250. *(Michael Mensing)*

Looking in the other direction from the previous picture, we see a Longsight 'Britannia' 4–6–2, no. 70031 *Byron*, in charge of the 10.20 a.m. London Euston–Manchester London Road approaching Prestbury on 27 March 1959. (*Michael Mensing*)

On 6 June 1953, south of Prestbury, a Stanier 2–6–4 tank, no. 42616, tackles the rising gradient at the head of the 4.20 p.m. Manchester London Road–Stoke. (*J.D. Darby*)

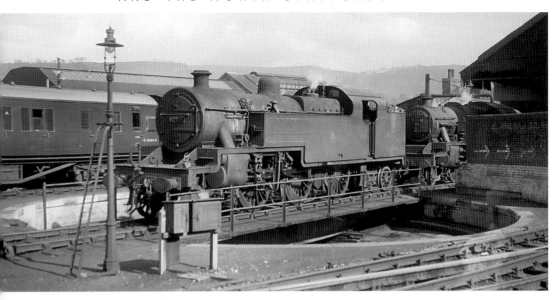

Macclesfield motive power depot was situated close to Hibel Road station and housed exclusively Fowler 2–6–4 tank engines in the 1950s. No. 42347 is seen on the gas-lit turntable at Macclesfield shed with a Stanier 2–6–4 tank, no. 42542, behind on 9 April 1960. The shed closed in 1961 and Hibel Road station, once used by many of the Manchester–London Euston expresses, shared the same fate when all trains used the former Macclesfield Central. (*Kidderminster Railway Museum*)

North Rode was the next station south of Macclesfield and it was here that the line to Leek and Uttoxeter branched away. A Longsight 'Silver Jubilee' 4–6–0, no. 45644 *Howe*, has just passed through the station and is approaching the junction with the 8.00 a.m. Colne–London Euston on 30 September 1959. The Colne portion of the train travelled via Blackburn, Bolton and Manchester Victoria and then made its way through the eastern suburbs of Manchester to Stockport where it joined the 10.00 a.m. from Manchester London Road for the journey to London Euston. (*Michael Mensing*)

Heading north at North Rode station, a Fowler 2–6–4 tank, no. 42304, emerges from the shadows with a freight that was mainly composed of coal wagons on 30 September 1959 at about 10.58 a.m. The engine had only recently moved to Longsight depot from Willesden. *(Michael Mensing)*

In this final view of the Manchester–London route via Stoke, we see an unrebuilt 'Patriot', no. 45520 *Llandudno*, with a stopping train near Astbury, south of Congleton, on 7 August 1954. This engine was based at Longsight depot, Manchester, for much of the 1950s. *(T. Noble/David Chatfield Collection)*

The main line via Stoke was part of the North Staffordshire Railway territory between Macclesfield and Colwich but that company reached into Cheshire by way of mainly rural lines. For instance, the NSR route between North Rode on the main line, north of Congleton, and Uttoxeter, served Leek and enjoyed freight receipts from local quarries but passenger traffic was light and the line was eventually closed. Only a small section of this line entered Cheshire and the one station within the county boundary, at Bosley, is seen here on 9 May 1959 with a Fowler 2–6–4 tank, no. 42369, leaving with the 3.44 p.m. Macclesfield–Uttoxeter. (*A.C. Gilbert*)

A further NSR branch ran from Stoke, through Biddulph, to join the Manchester–Stoke main line just north of Congleton, with a spur that led to a goods depot serving the town. On 30 May 1964, after closure, a special train was run along the line and Stanier class 5 4–6–0, no. 45020, is seen at the Congleton Goods terminus with the main line in the distance crossing over the Macclesfield Canal on the viaduct to the left and spanning the goods line by the viaduct in the centre of the picture. (*Alec Swain/ www.transporttreasury.co.uk*)

Further North Staffordshire Railway routes from Stoke made connections with the LNWR main lines at Sandbach and Crewe. These routes split near Lawton station and in this view of an LMS 'Crab' 2–6–0, no. 42727, in charge of an RCTS (West Midlands) 'St George' Railtour, the train passes the site of Lawton station, near Alsager, and approaches the junction with the Crewe–Stoke line on 23 April 1966 at 6.45 p.m. (*Michael Mensing*)

Services from Stoke via Alsager, on the former North Staffordshire line, brought Fowler 2–6–4 tank engines to Crewe on a regular basis. Here we see no. 42355 of Macclesfield shed approaching Crewe on 23 July 1959. (*Alec Swain/www.transporttreasury.co.uk*)

7

Around Crewe

When the GJR opened their line on 4 July 1837 from Warrington to Birmingham, Crewe was an insignificant stop near the village of Monks Coppenhall. Its significance grew when the Chester & Crewe Railway opened on 1 October 1840, thereby giving Crewe junction status. That status grew with the opening of another line from Manchester on 10 August 1842 by the Manchester & Birmingham Railway.

In the following year the first buildings at Crewe Works opened, and in 1845 the first locomotive, *Columbine*, was built for its owner, the GJR, soon to become part of the newly-formed LNWR. The works grew massively throughout the nineteenth century and such was the scale of the complex that it is reputed to have become the first factory in the world to manufacture steel on a commercial scale following the installation in 1864 of a Bessemer converter. In 1851 there were 649 employees in the works and railway shed but just over fifty years later there were in excess of 10,000 men. Locomotive building continued until 1958 when BR class 9F 2–10–0, no. 92250, became the last of a long line of steam locomotives, exceeding 7,000. The production of diesel locomotives continued but as the railway network contracted and locomotive building declined so did the fortunes of the works. Becoming part of British Rail Engineering Ltd, it was later sold off and fell into different ownerships owing to mergers and takeovers. Much of the site on which the works stood has been sold off for alternative uses while the works itself is a mere shadow of its former self.

Crewe station grew substantially throughout the nineteenth century and underwent a major development between 1903 and 1906 when it acquired an additional island platform and goods lines were built at a low level, burrowing below the land to the west of the station. These avoiding lines took freight to and from the Manchester and Liverpool lines clear of the station. Further modernisation coincided with electrification in the 1960s and then a major resignalling and track remodelling project between 1983 and 1985 culminated in the total closure of the station for a few weeks. Signalling was then handled by a new control centre at North Junction while the former LMS box became part of the then Crewe Railway Heritage site.

As well as the large works, there were two principal sheds and a small sub shed. Crewe North, code 5A, lay immediately north and west of the station and handled express passenger locomotives. Crewe South, coded 5B, lay to the south of the station in between the Shrewsbury and London lines. It handled mainly freight locomotives, many of which would have been engaged in train movements into and out of the huge Basford Hall marshalling yard, south of the shed. Both sheds had allocations of in excess of one hundred locomotives at one time or another. A third shed at Gresty Lane, on the north side of the Shrewsbury line, was a sub-shed of Wellington and was primarily used by GWR locomotives.

We return to Crewe, the hub of Cheshire's railways, via the West Coast Main Line. The two pictures above and below were taken at the point where the Cheshire countryside gives way to the extensive sidings at Basford Hall, about two miles south of the town and they show Stanier 'Princess Coronation' 4–6–2, no. 46248 *City of Leeds*, at the head of the 11.45 a.m. London Euston–Morecambe and Workington, in the process of overtaking the 1.45 p.m. Birmingham New Street–Liverpool Lime Street express on 15 July 1961. *(Michael Mensing)*

We begin at Crewe with a long trip down memory lane, to the early days of the LMS, when one of the new 'Royal Scot' 4–6–0s, no. 6139 *Ajax* (later renamed *The Welch Regiment*), approaches Crewe from the north with the Up 'Royal Scot' service, in 1928. In the distance, above the locomotive, is a signal gantry spanning the lines to Manchester. The picture was taken from the footbridge. *(C.A.J. Nevett/ Kidderminster Railway Museum)*

Much had changed in the twenty-five years that separates this view from that of the previous picture of the 'Royal Scot' express. Here the train seen approaching Crewe from the north, behind, on this occasion is 'Princess Coronation', no. 46221 *Queen Elizabeth*, on 22 July 1953. The Holyhead line veers away to the left in front of the signal-box. It is easy to see why there were speed restrictions in place around the station approaches. *(David Chatfield)*

In this picture taken in about 1949, 'Princess Coronation' Pacific, no. 46230 *Duchess of Buccleuch*, has emerged from Crewe Works after overhaul in BR blue livery and with 'British Railways' written on the tender. It stands on the no.1 Down through line at Crewe station and is seen from the footbridge linking the former platform 1 to Crewe North shed. The road entrance to Crewe station can be seen above the locomotive, which is waiting to take charge of a northbound express at about midday. No. 46230 was the first of its class to be built without streamlining. *(The Stephenson Locomotive Society)*

It is a late date for steam on a principal named train but here is a rebuilt 'Patriot', no. 45512 *Bunsen*, with the northbound 'Mid-day Scot' departing at 4.20 p.m. from Crewe on 23 August 1964. *(Peter Fitton)*

A 'Princess Coronation', no. 46238 *City of Carlisle*, awaits the 1.25 p.m. Euston–Perth on 25 March 1964. It will take over this train and depart at 4.40 p.m. and work, probably, as far as Carlisle, where it was based at the time. *(Peter Fitton)*

The 'Royal Scot' stands at a multiple aspect signal at Crewe station on 2 June 1953, the day of Queen Elizabeth II's Coronation, and hence the special crown headboard on the front of 'Royal Scot' 4–6–0, no. 46153 *The Royal Dragoon. (R.J. Leonard/Kidderminster Railway Museum)*

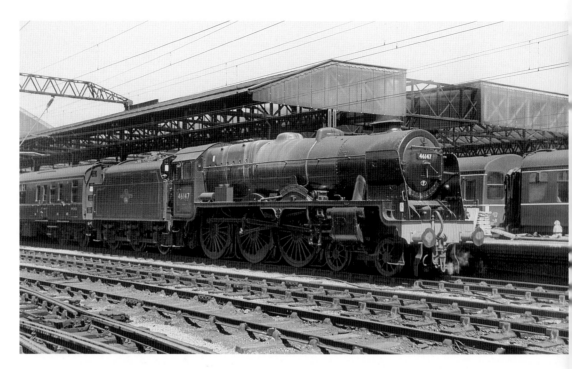

A 'Royal Scot', no. 46147 *The Northamptonshire Regiment*, based at Sheffield Millhouses depot, is seen at Crewe on 6 July 1961. Judging by the engine's condition, it may be on a running-in turn before returning to its Yorkshire base. *(Alec Swain/www.transporttreasury.co.uk)*

A GWR 'Manor' 4–6–0, no. 7809 *Childrey Manor*, of Oswestry depot, waits at one of Crewe's south bay platforms prior to working the 7.45 p.m. service to Whitchurch on 19 September 1961. *(Michael Mensing)*

An LMS 'Jinty' 0–6–0 tank, no. 47523, shunts vans at Crewe station in March 1953. The front number plate appears to be the old LMS number. *(David Chatfield)*

This pre-war scene taken at the south end of Crewe station, shows an LNWR 'Prince of Wales' 4–6–0, no. 25775, in LMS livery awaiting its next turn on 2 September 1938. Only three of this class, introduced by Bowen-Cooke in 1911, survived into BR days, but these did not include no. 25775. *(J.D. Darby)*

Before moving on to the locomotive sheds it is worth looking briefly at the Crewe avoiding lines, a speciality of the London North Western Railway. The LNWR's first attempt at building a flyover, in order to avoid the possibilities of congestion, was put into practice at Weaver Junction, in Cheshire. At Crewe, a junction where there was a large amount of freight as well as passenger traffic, the LNWR built freight lines that burrowed under the West Coast Main Line. On the west side of Crewe, a Bowen-Cooke 0–8–0, no. 49404, hauls a train in the direction of Crewe South on 27 March 1960. At a higher level and nearer to the station stands a Fowler 4F 0–6–0. (*Alec Swain/www.transporttreasury.co.uk*)

In the year before its closure, Crewe North shed is host to 'Royal Scot' 4–6–0, no. 46155 *The Lancer*, and its more modern counterpart, 'Britannia' 4–6–2, no. 70028 *Royal Star*, on 25 March 1964. (*Peter Fitton*)

A Llandudno Junction 'Silver Jubilee' 4–6–0, no. 45583 *Assam*, rests in between duties in Crewe North's semi-circular roundhouse on 23 February 1961. *(Peter Fitton)*

A Stanier 2–6–4 tank, no. 42152, in unlined livery, stands at the coaling tower at Crewe North on 21 August 1964 having been to the works for a service and repaint. Behind the tank engine is a Britannia 4–6–2, no. 70018 *Flying Dutchman*. *(Peter Fitton)*

Below the coal and ash plants at Crewe North on 23 February 1961 stand two 'Patriot' 4–6–0s, one of them, no. 45522 *Prestatyn*, in rebuilt form and the other, no. 45546 *Fleetwood*, unrebuilt. No. 45522 is from Kentish Town shed and has almost certainly paid a works visit. No. 45546 is closer to home, being allocated to Warrington Dallam. *(Peter Fitton)*

A 'Princess Coronation' 4–6–2, no. 46250 *City of Lichfield*, is in clean condition at Crewe North on 25 March 1964, despite being six months away from withdrawal, along with its remaining classmates. To the right of the Pacific is a BR class 4 2–6–4 tank, no. 80080, which survives today in preservation. *(Peter Fitton)*

GWR locomotives were a daily sight at Crewe and LNER motive power could be seen on a regular basis but to see examples from three regions together was less common. At Crewe North on 23 August 1964, an LNER B1 4–6–0, no. 61224, from Wakefield depot takes centre stage. To the rear of the B1 is a GWR 'Hall' 4–6–0, no. 6922 Burton Hall, of Shrewsbury depot, and to the right of the B1 stands an LMS class 5 4–6–0, no. 45116, of Llandudno Junction. (Peter Fitton)

The massive proportions of a Stanier 'Princess Royal' 4–6–2, no. 46206 Princess Marie Louise, can be seen to good effect in this view at Crewe North in March 1953. (David Chatfield)

In this final view of Crewe North shed, an un-rebuilt 'Royal Scot' 4–6–0, no. 6155 *The Lancer*, in fading LMS livery, is seen in the company of a Stanier 2–6–4 tank with a BR number and LMS emblazoned on its tank on 9 May 1948. *(J.D. Darby)*

Crewe South was primarily a freight depot but outlasted its counterpart to the north of Crewe station by two years. Two examples of the common LMS shunting locomotives, the 'Jinty' 0–6–0 tanks, seen all over the London Midland Region, are caught on camera at Crewe South with no. 47399 in the company of sister engine, no. 47354, on 23 August 1964. *(Peter Fitton)*

Another of the LMS workhorses was the 4F 0–6–0, of both Midland and LMS varieties. No. 43947 is one of the older Midland types and is seen on 23 August 1964. *(Peter Fitton)*

During its final year, Crewe South receives a visitor from Patricroft depot in the shape of BR class 5 4–6–0, no. 73131, on 12 March 1967. This particular engine is one of its class fitted with Caprotti valve gear. *(John Hilton)*

One of the more interesting aspects of visits to Crewe Works was the spotting of works shunters. For example, the Webb 0–6–0 saddle tank, no. 3323, designed for the LNWR, was a Crewe Works shunter for many years. It was out of use when seen on 28 March 1954 and scrapped shortly afterwards. It retained its LNWR number while at the works. *(David Chatfield)*

Another former LNWR saddle tank (though with an appearance more akin to a pannier tank), was the Webb 0–4–2 version, no. 47862, of 1901 vintage, used as a works shunter and photographed on 28 March 1954. *(David Chatfield)*

The sight of a Caledonian Railway locomotive in Cheshire would have been unheard of at one time but 0–4–0 saddle tank, no. 56032, was based at Crewe Works for a while. Note that the coal supply is stored on a ledge in front of the cab although these locomotives sometimes carried a wooden wagon with a separate supply of coal. The cab is being used by an engine man taking a break with his newspaper on 17 September 1955. *(RAS Marketing)*

Lancashire & Yorkshire Railway motive power could be seen at Crewe Works in the form of Aspinall 0–6–0 saddle tanks and the 0–6–0 3F freight engines. Both examples can be seen at the works in May 1954 with no. 52216 in ex-works condition in the foreground, and two 0–6–0 saddle tanks in the background including no. 11368, which would later become a Horwich Works shunter. *(T. Noble/ David Chatfield Collection)*

As well as building new locomotives, the erecting shops were used for overhauling. On 18 December 1966, locomotives in various stages of overhaul are, from left to right, the frames of 'Britannia' class 4–6–2, no. 70013 *Oliver Cromwell*, the frames and boilers of BR class 9F 2–10–0s, nos 92203 and 92220 *Evening Star*, and the boiler of Gresley A4 Pacific, no. 60007 *Sir Nigel Gresley*. *Evening Star* was the last steam locomotive to be built for British Railways but this took place at Swindon Works in 1960. The last locomotive to be built at Crewe was of the same class, no. 92250, which left the works on 15 December 1958. *Oliver Cromwell* was the last steam locomotive to be overhauled and this is taking place at Crewe Works where it left on 2 February 1967. *(Peter Fitton)*

A 'Princess Coronation', no. 46239 *City of Chester*, is seen in shop grey in August 1954 on the way to completion of its overhaul. *(T. Noble/ David Chatfield Collection)*

A rebuilt 'Patriot' 4–6–0, no. 45527 *Southport*, has been repainted and waits to be reunited with its tender. Behind *Southport* is an unidentified and unrebuilt 'Patriot'. *(T. Noble/David Chatfield Collection)*

In this view of the pioneer 'Patriot' 4–6–0, no. 45500 *Patriot*, in May 1957, the locomotive has been outshopped and is ready to return to its home depot at Carlisle Upperby. Designed by Fowler in 1930 for the LMS, this locomotive incorporated the original wheels of a 'Claughton' 4–6–0. *(T. Noble/David Chatfield Collection)*

Less than four years later, *Patriot* returns to Crewe Works, initially marked for overhaul but subsequently scrapped. It is seen on 23 February 1961 with a Newton Heath shed plate in the company of a BR class 9F 2–10–0. The class 9F is attached to a Fowler tender, possibly that belonging to *Patriot*. *(Peter Fitton)*

Standing outside the paint shops after overhaul at Crewe Works on 23 February 1961 is Stanier class 4 2–6–4 tank, no. 42608, of Birkenhead shed. Behind it are two new Sulzer Type 4 diesel locomotives. *(Peter Fitton)*

Although the North Staffordshire Railway played a significant part in the railway activities in the eastern half of the county, none of that company's locomotive stock survived into BR ownership. In fact, the last engine was withdrawn in 1939. It is fitting therefore that at least one example appears in this album and it is one of the more familiar NSR locomotives, the L class 3F 0–6–2 tank engines, no. 2267, at Crewe Works yard in April 1935. Fortunately, a sister engine, no. 2271, survives today in preservation having been sold by the LMS to Lancashire Associated Collieries. *(RAS Marketing)*

One of the successful Webb 0–6–2 tank engines for the LNWR ends its life at its birthplace in August 1954. Three hundred of these engines were built at Crewe between 1881 and 1896 and fifty survived as BR stock. No. 58921 was an Edge Hill, Liverpool, locomotive and a sister engine, no. 58926, was preserved following withdrawal in January 1958. *(T. Noble/ David Chatfield Collection)*

In a depressing, run-down corner of Crewe works, the first of the Webb 'Coal Engine' 0–6–0s, no. 58321, is in the process of being broken up on 8 August 1953 after a lifespan of nearly seventy years. Its dome lies to one side, together with corrugated sheeting from the shed. Such neglect today would, no doubt, attract the interest of health and safety inspectors. *(T. Noble/David Chatfield Collection)*

It is the end of the road for Webb 'Coal Engine' 0–6–0, no. 58343, at Crewe Works on 8 August 1953. It was one of the last two of its class to be withdrawn, bringing extinction to a successful class. They were built from 1873 at Crewe Works and over the next twenty years 500 were built, of which nearly half passed into LMS ownership. *(T. Noble/David Chatfield Collection)*

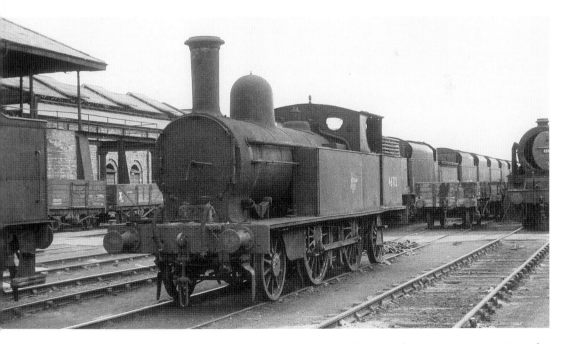

Another old LNWR engine awaits its fate at the place of its birth more than sixty years earlier. The Webb 2–4–2 passenger tank engines were built from 1890 and no. 46712 was one of the last survivors when seen at Crewe Works in August 1954. The last examples of this class were withdrawn in the following year. *(T. Noble/ David Chatfield Collection)*

A Beyer-Garratt 2–6–6–2, no. 47984, is at Crewe Works in August 1954 awaiting overhaul but the first withdrawals of this class of thirty-three took place in the following year and all were gone by 1958. The rapid decline of these locomotives was due to their high maintenance costs coupled with the introduction of the BR class 9F 2–10–0s. *(T. Noble/David Chatfield Collection)*

The last survivor of the L&YR 2–4–2 tank engines, designed by Aspinall, waits to be scrapped at Crewe Works on 10 December 1961. Like the LNWR 0–6–2 tank engines these were a successful design and a numerous class. One has been preserved but no. 50850, which spent its last few months as a station pilot engine at Southport, was not so lucky. It is, perhaps, surprising that the locomotive was scrapped at Crewe instead of at the former L&YR works at Horwich. *(Peter Fitton)*

A steam test is conducted on 'Silver Jubilee' 4–6–0, no. 45577 *Bengal*, at Crewe Works on 25 March 1964. It appears that the locomotive failed its test as it was not repaired and subsequently withdrawn in the summer of that year. *(Peter Fitton)*

8

Decline of Steam

During the 1950s several changes took place to mark the beginning of the end for steam. The growing trend towards car ownership and road haulage was accompanied by the modernisation programme on the railways resulting in a wave of new diesel shunters, followed by the first main line diesel locomotives to appear in significant quantities, and the spread of the diesel (and later electric) multiple unit. Electric traction had replaced steam on the Woodhead route in 1954, bringing to an end the daily arrival of LNER express passenger types. The loss of further passenger services such as that between Whitchurch and Tattenhall Junction in 1957 came with the first significant railway closure between Hooton and West Kirkby on the Wirral in 1956.

In 1960 the last steam locomotive was built while the older locomotives were consigned to scrapyards in greater numbers. Electrification of the Manchester and Liverpool routes to Crewe was completed in 1960 and 1962 respectively. In 1963 the Beeching Report was published with one of its proposals to concentrate the carriage of passengers and goods at speed between the main centres, thus finding an echo in the original GJR proposal for its trunk route through Cheshire. This period saw massive reductions in goods yards and passenger stations together with the complete closure of lines; some CLC routes lost their passenger services and all that was left of the former North Staffordshire network was the Crewe–Stoke line via Alsager and the main line from Stoke to Manchester as far as Macclesfield. Even the Midland Railway main line through Cheadle Heath lost its services.

The decline in the traditional industries such as coal in the 1960s added to the carnage on the railways. Of the larger stations, those at Stockport Tiviot Dale, Birkenhead Woodside (together with the main line services to Paddington) and Chester Northgate were the main casualties. All of the twelve motive power depots in Cheshire (including the sub-shed at Gresty Lane) that came under BR operation in 1948, survived until 1960. The former GWR depot at Chester closed in that year when Cheshire lost its allocation of GWR locomotives although they still worked into Chester as well as Crewe. Chester Northgate shed closed in the same year while Macclesfield shed closed in 1961 and Alsager in the following year. Gresty Lane shed closed in 1963 as did Bidston, marking the end of Cheshire's allocation of LNER types. In 1965 Crewe North shed closed, by which time the allocation of express locomotives comprised Stanier class 5 4–6–0s and 'Britannia' Pacifics. In 1967, Crewe South, Birkenhead and Chester sheds closed their doors. The closure of Birkenhead depot coincided with the last steam-hauled train of hopper wagons between Bidston Dock and John Summers & Sons Ltd steelworks at Shotton on 6 November 1967. BR class 9F no. 92203 handled the last train and has since been preserved.

Northwich and Stockport sheds survived until 1968 and Stockport's depot was the last to succumb in May 1968. Steam operation in Britain ended on 11 August 1968 with the last special train. In 1955, there were about 18,500 locomotives and over the course of the next five years a further 500 were built. That this number was scrapped over a period of thirteen years gives an indication of how savage was the destruction and how swift the decline of the steam locomotive.

The fires have been extinguished for the last time and the snow on the ground emphasises this cold reality as locomotives stand in the scrap line awaiting the breaker's torch. At the front of the line is a WD 2–8–0, no. 90356, followed by a 'Royal Scot' 4–6–0, no. 46131 *The Royal Warwickshire Regiment*. The date is 18 November 1962 and no. 46131 is among the first batch of its class to be withdrawn. *(Peter Fitton)*

By the time this picture was taken on 3 August 1964, withdrawals of motive power had affected almost every class of locomotive including all pre-BR types. Those classes built in large numbers such as the Stanier class 5s and class 8s would inevitably predominate and at Chester General three of the class 5s can be seen around the grouping of signals. No. 45091, of Llandudno Junction, arrives from Manchester with an express for the North Wales coast while other members of the class are held at signals. Note the brazier at the base of the water column that was used on cold winter days to prevent the water from freezing. *(Tom Heavyside)*

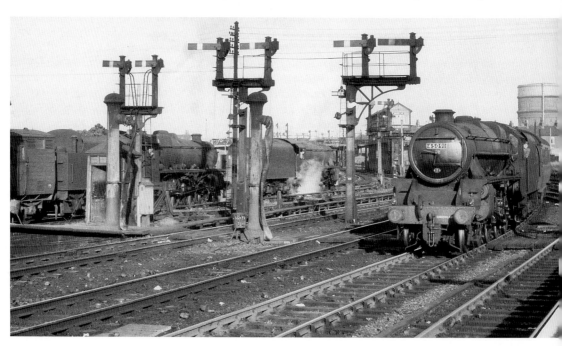

Working in an environment with coal, oil and ash around, and subject to the vagaries of the weather was far from pleasant but thousands of railwaymen took this in their stride. At Birkenhead shed on 18 February 1966, an impression of this environment is conveyed as a WD 2–8–0, no. 90351, and BR class 9F 2–10–0, no. 92157, await their next duties. *(Tom Heavyside)*

Another look at Birkenhead shed where many locomotives are in steam in this busy scene featuring three locomotives types – Stanier 8F 2–8–0s, BR class 9 2–10–0s and a WD 2–8–0. To the right of the retaining wall is Stanier 8F 2–8–0, no. 48613, while BR class 9F 2–10–0, no. 92048, can be seen beyond the lighting pole towards the right. To the left of no. 92048 is a WD 2–8–0, no. 90351. After Bidston shed closed in 1963, Birkenhead depot provided the motive power for the heavy iron ore trains that ran between Bidston Dock and Shotwick Sidings, serving the John Summers & Sons Ltd steelworks. The last of these steam-hauled trains ran behind 9F no. 92203 on 6 November 1967 and Birkenhead shed closed to steam. *(Tom Heavyside)*

Returning to Chester from Birkenhead, we see an LMS class 4 2–6–4 tank in charge of a Paddington express as far as Chester. Stanier engine, no. 42647, arrives at Hooton with the 11.45 a.m. Birkenhead–Paddington on 22 August 1966. (*Tom Heavyside*)

By 1966 only the 'Silver Jubilees' of the ex-LMS express locomotive types survived. At Chester shed no. 45647 *Sturdee* is coaled up and in steam on 18 February 1966. (*Tom Heavyside*)

Three different classes of locomotives can be seen in this picture. At centre stage is a Stanier class 5 4–6–0, no. 45231, of Chester shed, with a train for Wolverhampton. A few years earlier, such a train would have been hauled by a GWR 4–6–0. No. 45231 is one of its class that has been preserved. To the right is a Stanier class 4 2–6–4 tank, no. 42616, with express headlamps suggesting that it is waiting to take over a Birkenhead train. On the left, behind the class 5 is a Stanier class 8F 2–8–0. *(Tom Heavyside)*

One of the ubiquitous Stanier class 5 4–6–0s, no. 45238, slows for signals as it runs along the centre road at Chester General with a parcels train on 22 August 1966. *(Tom Heavyside)*

A 'Britannia' 4–6–2, no. 70011 (formerly *Hotspur*), is reduced to hauling a goods train such as this Up freight at Preston Brook, south of Warrington, on 8 July 1967. By this time, the remaining passenger duties for steam engines in this area were handled by Stanier class 5s or 'Britannias'. *(Tom Heavyside)*

One of the many railtours that were organised in the 1960s crosses the Shropshire Union Canal on the approach to Chester. A Stanier class 5 4–6–0, no. 44680, is in charge of a London Paddington–Birkenhead special train in July 1967. *(Tony Oldfield)*

Only two sheds in Cheshire handled a steam allocation in 1968. At Northwich, two Stanier 8Fs are at rest between the depot and the station in February 1968, a month before closure. An unidentified 2–8–0 is in steam beyond no. 48224 of Patricroft depot. (*Tom Heavyside*)

It is almost the end for Stockport shed and there is little activity among the steam engines on 30 March 1968. A Stanier class 5 4–6–0, no. 44855, and Stanier class 8F 2–8–0, no. 48549, are prominent in this view of the depot with the Manchester–London line beyond. The shed was the last in Cheshire to end its association with steam locomotives when it closed its doors to steam in May. (*Tom Heavyside*)

A cleaner's eye view of a Stanier 8F 2–8–0, no. 48745, at Stockport Edgeley shed on 30 March 1968. Raking out the fire and ash from under the steam locomotive was one of the least pleasant tasks undertaken around the shed. The products of that work appear to have been left in the channel in front of the locomotive, while some of the tools have been dumped by the side of the rails. There is a sense from looking at this scene that morale in this industry at that time was low. *(Tom Heavyside)*

A line-up of Stanier locomotives at Stockport Edgeley shed on 13 April 1968 includes two class 5 4–6–0s nearest to the camera. Beyond nos 44855 and 45027 is a Stanier 8F 2–8–0. *(Tom Heavyside)*

In this last look at Skelton Junction, a Stanier class 5 4–6–0, no. 45282, is approaching the junction with a coal train, possibly for Fiddlers Ferry power station, on 27 April 1968. The signal is indicating that the train will take the line through Broadheath, further evidence that the power station may be the destination. *(Tom Heavyside)*

A feature of the last few months of steam operation was the enthusiasts' special, often with two locomotives in charge as an added attraction. Such a combination makes an impressive exit from Stalybridge in the north-eastern corner of Cheshire. Two of Patricroft's allocation of BR class 5 4–6–0s, nos 73050 and 73069, storm away from this mill town on a tour around Lancashire via Huddersfield, the Calder Valley line and the Copy Pit route to Burnley on 27 April 1968. *(Gavin Morrison)*

A final view of steam in BR ownership shows 'Britannia' 4–6–2, no. 70013 *Oliver Cromwell*, at Stockport Edgeley shed on 13 April 1968 as it prepares to leave for the station to take charge of a returning Edinburgh–Stafford special train. Unlike most of the surviving locomotives at this time, it was kept in pristine condition and was one of the four locomotives used on the very last steam special on 11 August 1968 that brought the curtain down on the steam era. The locomotive was subsequently preserved. *(Tom Heavyside)*

Preserved Steam

Preservation can be said to have started long ago in Cheshire when the LNWR and the LMS set aside historic locomotives such as *Columbine*, the first engine to be built at Crewe Works, *Cornwall*, built at the works in 1847 to a design by Francis Trevithick, and *Hardwicke*, famous for its part in the 'Races to the North' of 1895. *Hardwicke's* most famous run began at Crewe and passed through Cheshire on its way to Carlisle. The locomotive was one of F.W. Webb's most successful designs. These engines were kept at the paint shops in Crewe works for many years.

After the end of steam operations on BR in 1968, a 'Return to Steam' special ran in the Midlands in 1971, paving the way for a return of steam power along prescribed routes, including the Hope Valley line to Sheffield and the line from Chester towards Shrewsbury and Newport. The period saw the use of Northwich shed as a servicing point for preserved locomotives on these trains. This shed was also used by some engines making their way to the 'Rocket 150' Celebrations in 1980 when the opening of the Liverpool–Manchester Railway was commemorated.

In 1987 a major event took place with the opening of the Crewe Heritage Centre (now The Railway Age) by Her Majesty the Queen. The main exhibition building was constructed in the 'V' of the Holyhead and Glasgow lines. In the following year steam trains were run to Chester, Shrewsbury and back to Crewe, via Whitchurch using 'Princess Royal' 4–6–2 *Princess Elizabeth*. These runs were a prelude to the use of steam on the Holyhead route in 1989 when the 'North Wales Coast Express' ran through the summer of that year and since then. Crewe, fittingly, has become a prominent base for steam locomotives while steam workings have covered much ground within the county including both the Chester–Manchester lines and up and down the West Coast Main Line.

Thankfully, steam appears to have a secure future in Cheshire.

Since the end of steam on BR's scheduled services, preserved locomotives have travelled extensively over the BR network. In the early days of preservation, steam was confined to certain designated routes but there has been a considerable relaxation of these restrictions over the years. However, because of the higher speeds being achieved by modern traction, it is likely that the paths for steam will become more restricted again. The route through Stockport–Altrincham–Northwich–Chester has been a popular one, especially when Northwich shed provided opportunities for servicing steam locomotives. A Southern Railway 'Merchant Navy', no. 35028 *Clan Line*, leaves Altrincham station, southern end of the electric line to Manchester, on a Hereford–Guide Bridge special on 28 April 1979. (*Tom Heavyside*)

A BR class 4 2–6–4 tank, no. 80079, based at the Severn Valley Railway, is watered at Northwich shed. A hosepipe is used instead of the old tower or column and the occasion is an open day on 18 May 1980. (*Tom Heavyside*)

The Rocket 150 Celebrations at Rainhill in 1980 involved a lot of organising so that those steam locomotives taking part could reach the venue with the minimum of disruption. Northwich shed was used for intermediate stabling of engines including Gresley A4 Pacific, no. 4498 *Sir Nigel Gresley*, and Stanier class 5 4–6–0, no. 5000, here being hauled by a class 25 diesel, no. 25294, across Frodsham viaduct over the Weaver Navigation. The ensemble is making its way to Bold power station on 20 May 1980. (*Tom Heavyside*)

A former Southern Railway 'King Arthur' 4–6–0, no. 777 *Sir Lamiel*, storms out of Chester with a returning special to Hull on 14 May 1983. Earlier in the day it had worked from Hereford to Chester on a 'Welsh Marches Express'. *Sir Lamiel* is taking the route towards Manchester while the Crewe lines approach the camera. (*Tom Heavyside*)

Another view of Southern Railway 'Merchant Navy' 4–6–2, no. 35028 *Clan Line*, as it arrives at Chester from the west with a special on 29 September 1984. Part of the former Chester shed can just be seen on the right while the lines towards Birkenhead curve sharply round to the right. *(Tom Heavyside)*

One of the most famous of all locomotives, Gresley A3 4–6–2, no. 4472 *Flying Scotsman*, departs from Chester station for Manchester on 29 September 1984 in front of a large crowd of enthusiasts gathered on the platforms. *(Tom Heavyside)*

At the Crewe Heritage
Centre Festival of
2 August 1987, an
impressive line-up of
locomotives can be seen,
including, at the far end,
industrial tank engine
Bellerophon, Stanier
'Princess Royal' 4–6–2,
no. 6201 *Princess
Elizabeth*, BR class 8
4–6–2, no. 71000 *Duke of
Gloucester*, Stanier class
8F 2–8–0, no. 48151, and
two diesel locomotives.
To the left is the historic
Lion with replica
Liverpool & Manchester
Railway coaches.
(Tom Heavyside)

Another view of the Crewe Heritage Centre Festival shows *Lion* taking centre stage. Probably the
oldest working locomotive in the world, *Lion* was nearly 150 years old when this picture was taken.
Although the coaches represent the same period, they are in fact replicas built in modern times.
(Tom Heavyside)

To celebrate the centenary of Lever Brothers' Port Sunlight factory on the Wirral, a shuttle service was run on their private industrial line with locomotives at either end of the train. A GWR 2–6–2 tank, no. 4566, on loan from the Severn Valley Railway, is seen on 30 April 1988, the first of three days of shuttle services. At the other end was an LMS 'Jinty' 0–6–0. (*Tom Heavyside*)

Stanier 8F 2–8–0, no. 48773, approaches Northwich from Chester on 1 February 1992 while en route from its base at the Severn Valley Railway to the Keighley & Worth Valley Railway. Beyond the signal, the branch to Middlewich and Sandbach diverges. *(Tom Heavyside)*

Princess Coronation' 4–6–2, no. 46229 *Duchess of Hamilton*, arrives at Chester station with the returning North Wales Coast Express' from Holyhead to Crewe on 30 June 1991. *(Tom Heavyside)*

In this final view of steam in Cheshire we see 'Princess Coronation' 4–6–2, no. 46229 *Duchess of Hamilton* at Crewe having returned to the West Coast Main Line. It is at the head of an enthusiasts' special, complete with 'The Caledonian' headboard, to Carlisle on 3 October 1995. *(David Packer)*